2(

LUCY'S RAINBOW

LUCY'S RAINBOW

A Journey of Hope

JUDY HOPKINS
with Helen Porter

Authentic

First published 2011 by Authentic Media Limited
Presley Way, Crownhill, Milton Keynes, MK8 0ES
www.authenticmedia.co.uk

British Library Cataloguing in Publication Data

A catalogue record for this book is available from the British
Library

ISBN: 978-1-85078-954-3

Unless otherwise stated, Scripture quotations are taken from the
HOLY BIBLE, NEW INTERNATIONAL VERSION. Copyright ©
1973, 1978, 1984 by International Bible Society. Used by permission
of Hodder & Stoughton, a division of Hodder Headline Ltd. All
rights reserved. 'NIV' is a registered trademark of the International
Bible Society UK trademark number 1448790

Some names have been changed for the sake of privacy.

Frontispiece by Robert Goldsmith; Illustrations by Rachel Hopkins;
Photos edited by Beth Coppard
Cover photo of Lucy by Russell Hopkins
Cover Design by Paul Airy (www.designleft.co.uk)
Printed and bound in Great Britain by Cox and Wyman, Reading

**For my darling girls: Rachel who saw the
Rainbow
and Lucy who drew it**

Contents

Contents

RUSS

You carried the Moses basket to my car
To help me.
Your last gesture to me,
one of kindness
To lend us your own child's crib
So kind,
But also, to want to help and serve.

Little did we know then
That this would be our last goodbye.

As you turned and left
I hoped and prayed
That God would be merciful,
And that you would live.

How I wish we could have said
Something different to you that day,
But maybe God wanted us all to have hope and strength,
Hope till the end.

I think I felt bitter with God
That you died,
That our prayers were not answered.
A God of miracles
Could have done a miracle for you,
But chose not to.
Why?
I asked
Why?

You had everything to live for
A wife,
Two beautiful daughters,
They all adored you,
Why was your life cut so short?

I think now that I can understand a bit more,
God allows certain things to happen
Though not his will.
We live in a fallen world
Sad but it's a fact
We live here with both the good and the evil,
Life and death all around us
Suffering never far away.

I think I blamed you, God
For letting Russ die
Forgive me,
For I now see that death,
and it will come to us all one day,
Is the ultimate victory
For those who love you
And trust you.   Amen

Sue Trickey, July 2002

ACKNOWLEDGEMENTS

Thank you, Morag, for your support and encouragement as we worked through the book together. Happy times, hilarious moments and spontaneous meals out when our brains could take no more. It was such fun! Thank you, Helen, for the privilege of having your professional help over recent months to shape my book in preparation for publication. We sure have met some deadlines together! Thank you, Jackie, my lovely sister-in-law, for being there for me with all your help from the very beginning.

To Fiona Castle I give my thanks for your advice to 'go for it', before I even put pen to paper. Thank you, Carl, my writer friend, and Mollie, my godmother, for your interest in my book.

My appreciation to Prue and Ange for your timely help, and to all those involved in the publication, for your patience.

Thank you, Fi, for your conviction that my book would be published 'at the right time', and thank you, Ben and Chris, for keeping me focused. Thank you, Rob, for the beautiful painting.

I thank both sides of my family for your love and understanding throughout this period. To my loving father, my dear friend, Linda, and to all others who have supported me over the years in the raising of my girls and in the writing of my story, thank you.

Finally, thank you to all at Trinity Cheltenham who have prayed for me and who have encouraged me to pursue my God-given dream, *Lucy's Rainbow*.

To God be the glory.

Judy Hopkins
December 2010

FOREWORD

I first met Judy not long after the death of her husband, Russ, at such an early age, from leukaemia. I was immediately struck by her warm, friendly personality, and by the amazingly positive way she was dealing with her bereavement.

Her book reflects this positive yet searching attitude, as she describes the symptoms and treatment of her husband's illness. It is a compellingly honest read from the first chapter, incorporating the many emotions of bewilderment and loss, both for her and for her two young daughters.

She endorses the fact that everyone deals with grief in a different way and how her very real faith in Christ was her saving grace.

Throughout her story I also realized the value of friendship, as so many of Judy's friends rallied to support her, both during Russ's illness and after his death. I can only imagine she must *be* a friend to many, in order to engender such loving care in return!

Reverend Jim Graham spoke of there coming a time when we must give ourselves permission to stop our grieving. Judy eventually arrives at this place.

Through various struggles and setbacks, she provides hope for life, trusting the One who holds the future.

Fiona Castle,
Autumn 2010

1

INTRODUCTION

I made the short journey from home to Frenchay Hospital on autopilot, feeling nothing, seeing nothing, passing the hospital entrance without even registering the sleeping policemen on my mental radar.

Like a lightning bolt to the core of my being I understood that the man I married seven and a half years earlier might never walk again – realized that on top of his life-threatening leukaemia, he might be paralyzed, and that we might never make love again. I didn't admit to myself the unthinkable possibility: that he might even die.

As I parked the car and walked blankly into the maze leading to Russ's ward, I thought, 'What will he look like? Will he be able to move?' The previous night he had been so frightened that a ward nurse had phoned the hospital chaplain and asked him to make an emergency visit. Would he be even worse this evening?

When I reached the ward, I was stunned to find a scene of complete tranquillity. He lay on his bed, cupping his pocket Bible in his hands. Smiling, he said calmly, 'It's wonderful to see you.'

How could this be the frightened, anxious man who had been carried down three flights of stairs by porters yesterday morning? What on earth had happened to change him so dramatically? I steadied my legs, slid into the bedside chair and stared wide-eyed at my transformed husband.

He began, 'Something amazing happened to me last night. I saw myself in a dark tunnel and then realized that in front of me were the gates of hell. I found I had to keep on walking towards them, and when I reached the end of the tunnel, I felt terrified, as if I was about to be catapulted through those gates. But nothing happened. Suddenly I saw the cross, and Jesus was with me, saying, "You don't have to go there – nobody has to go there, because of what I did for you on the cross." When I heard those words I was filled with an overwhelming sense of peace. Seeing Jesus, and hearing him, made me feel utterly humble. Then he said, "Russ, I am in charge of your life."'

Russ leaned towards me earnestly, 'Judy, this is going to transform my ministry, and you've entered into it too.'

That night when I returned to our flat, I sank to my knees on the kitchen floor and poured out my heart to God. 'It doesn't matter how you use me Lord, as long as I'm where you want me to be,' I sobbed.

I felt something shift in the heavens that night, but I had no idea of the depths and agonies through which the journey was about to take me.

A TREE ON A HILL

Ever since leaving school, marriage and children were all I ever wanted. But for many years, I doubted this would happen to me.

It was late February 1982. I was 22, living in Cheltenham, training as a midwife, and I'd reached a low point in my life and relationships. One day I felt a desperate need to get out of the hospital. I took myself up Cleeve Hill, the ancient outcrop which stands close to the eastern part of town. As I climbed higher I thought, 'Here I am again, in this familiar place, alone, yet crying out for a deep and lasting relationship.'

When I reached the top of the hill I saw a lone tree. Its isolation struck a chord, and I called out to God, 'It's not fair! Everyone else has found someone, and I feel so lonely.'

The western view had opened up. I could see the hospital and the town becoming smaller and smaller beneath me, and I felt a sense of perspective beginning to take shape. Suddenly I realized that there was more to life than my unfulfilled longings. I sat down on the hillside beneath the tree and clasped my knees in my hands.

'I'm 22, Lord. Will I ever have children of my own?' I asked out loud: 'Will I ever have a fulfilling relationship?'

By the time I climbed back down to the city nothing external had actually changed, but I felt more peaceful inside, as if the thing I was yearning for was only just out of reach.

For many years leading up to that day, I'd lived a kind of double life – partly the insecure socialite crying out for affection, partly the sweet, smiling Judy who never did anything wrong. It scared me that I was often both people at once.

I had come to Cheltenham after deliberately choosing to leave all my friends in Cambridge, to put myself in a new situation to try to remove any distractions from becoming a Christian. I'd recently split from my latest boyfriend, who had made an accusation that was still ringing in my ears: 'Judy, other Christians' lives ring a lot truer than yours. You need to take a long, hard look at yourself.'

That really hurt me, but I knew he was right. I was living in two camps, and it was glaringly obvious that many aspects of my life didn't match up to what I knew was right as a Christian. I'd dipped in and out of churches, slipping away before anyone could engage me in conversation. I had been to hear Billy Graham, and even joined Christian groups, but didn't feel I belonged and always dropped out. I was refusing to commit my life, even though I knew that that was what I needed.

On my first Sunday evening in Cheltenham I decided to go to church, intending to find one in the town centre. But when I looked through my window and heard the local church bells, I felt strangely drawn. It was a cold and windy January evening, but I pulled my collar up around my neck and took the plunge.

There were less than ten in the congregation and the service was very formal, but I was really impressed by the lay preacher. He clearly believed what he was saying and seemed totally genuine. It was obvious to me that he knew God. So I went back, again and again. I joined the midweek Bible study group and did a pretty good job of convincing everyone I was a real Christian, all the time knowing inside that I was not. It was just the same as my simple childhood awareness of God when I used to write my diary to him, and the teenage enthusiasm for talking about God to the lads from my youth group in the pub when I knew I was partly living a lie.

One night in March 1982 I had a dream that my ex-boyfriend in Cambridge had become a Christian – a crazy idea as he hadn't seemed remotely inclined towards faith. But on my day off I jumped into my bright red and orange Vauxhall Viva – originally red, but every time I'd bumped it my dad and I fitted a replacement part from an orange Viva at the local scrap yard. I drove straight to my ex's lodgings and knocked on the door. His flatmate answered.

'Hi, I'm looking for Julian,' I said, feeling a little embarrassed as I hadn't seen him for ages.

'He's not here, Judy,' he laughed. 'He's probably out trying to convert somebody.'

My jaw dropped. I couldn't believe it. I rushed away from the flat and raced through the sixteenth-century college buildings where cheery daffodils were nodding their heads, until I reached the well-worn steps to Julian's college library. When I found him, we talked in a way we had never done before. To me he was the Mr Darcy to my Elizabeth, but as we talked late into the evening it became clear to both of us that our being together might not be part of God's agenda. We figured that if we were sincere about following him, we had to actually follow! It was a sorry and unhappy me that left the library and walked back to the car park.

As I drove back to Cheltenham, the reality of my own situation began to sink in. I began to take the long, hard look at myself that Julian had once recommended. And I didn't like what I saw.

My mind in turmoil, I looked back at the times of pain and confusion over the last six years.

I remembered how just a year before I'd left Cambridge I had walked down the mile-long road to the nurses' home alone after a late party. A Canadian guy I'd flirted with, dated and convinced myself was 'The One' had brushed me off and I was feeling hurt. I'd had one glass too many to drink, my shoe heel had broken off, and I was barefoot. It had been a wretched time, knowing I was a mess inside, torn between two different camps, trying to shut out the 'God' part or the 'me' part, and always failing.

As I faced up to the past, I admitted I'd known God was there all the time, that he was constant, and I couldn't keep running away from him. Since I was 13 I'd kept a booklet a friend had given to me because I was struck by the phrase, 'You're not a Turk because you wear a fez.' That comment had always bugged and nagged at me – wearing a fez doesn't make you a Turk, and going to church didn't make me a Christian.

And now I faced up to the fact that I knew I had the ability to attract some men, but this often led to confusion and heartbreak. I longed for love but was going about it in the wrong way. Every time a relationship ended I was hit by the fear that I would never meet Mr Right and get married. Everyone around me seemed to have the settled and secure relationship that I wanted for myself. I admitted that I had always kept God on the periphery of my life.

Memories came flooding back – some from childhood – a journey in the back of a friend's car when her father had quizzed me about my Christian faith. I tried to explain my belief and he had said, 'You think all this because you're young. When you're older, you'll see how you've been taken in.'

'But I'm not being taken in!' I retorted. That night I read in the Bible how Paul told Timothy not to let people look down on him because he was young, and I had known God was speaking to me and immediately felt better.

As I looked back, it was clear to see how I'd found it easy to trust God – I had a trusting nature. When I was about 12, I'd walked with my friend Beth across the fields to Stamford. As we neared the town, a youngish man approached and beckoned us to look at some flowers in the next field. Even though I knew never to speak to strangers, I went with him, while Beth, who was more astute than me, was tugging at my sleeve, whispering, 'Come away, Judy!' We ran for our lives with the man in pursuit, and blurted it all out to a policeman we saw in town.

Four years later I'd been walking near home when a car slowed down beside me and the middle-aged male driver called out, 'Can you show me the way to a café? It'll be easier if you hop in the car and show me.'

So I got in and directed him to my dad's shop close by, and the guy asked me out for supper. That evening my furious mum stood over me while I told him there would be no supper date.

As I drove back to Cheltenham, I accepted that throughout my early years God nourished my hunger to find meaning in life. I remembered the summer evening when I was no more than 10, lying in bed listening to other children still playing out in the street. I'd looked out of the window longingly and thought, 'We're born, we live, we die. What then? What's the point of life?'

Now I confessed that I'd known for a long time that I had a choice to make: To keep God on the edge, or ask him into the centre of my life. I had no idea what would happen with Julian, or whether I would ever get married at all. I had had a cross on the wall, and occasionally had taken it down when tempted to behave in a way that would not be God's best. Although I longed to be married, I decided that any future relationships would be run by different rules – God's rules. This was about absolute surrender. This was the deal.

Back at my nurses' home in Cheltenham late that night – 2 March 1982 – I took a radical step. Kneeling down beside my bed on my oval beige rug, I called out to God:

'I'm going to put you first in my life. And that means even if you want me to live in a mud hut in Africa and never get married – I will do it!'

I opened my eyes and decided to write down what I had said. That way it would be definite, and not go the way of other prayers that hadn't proved sincere. I knew that for me to write it down made it into a contract.

There was no clap of thunder or bolt of lightning as I went to sleep that night. But the next morning I opened my eyes and immediately picked up my Bible. I read in the book of James: 'What causes fights and quarrels among you? Don't they come from your desires that battle within you? You want something but don't get it' (Jas. 4:1). For the first time the words in the Bible jumped off the page as if they were written just for me. I felt elated and excited and wanted to read more and more and more.

Just then, the midwifery student from the room next door knocked and came in to talk about my hamster. It had found its way into her underwear drawer and eaten a corner of her nightie. I read her the Bible passage and tried to explain what it meant to me. But like so many people I tried to tell in the next few days, she seemed to think I was acting crazy.

I couldn't stop talking about how it felt to have Christ in my life. I was overflowing, like a dam that had burst! The whole of nature seemed to suddenly be in 3D, too. 'Look at that tree!' I exclaimed to two friends on the way to the shopping centre. 'Just look!' They did look – not at the tree but at each other, and I could tell they were wondering which planet I'd come from.

'Judy, the whole hospital's talking about you. Will you shut up!' blurted one of my friends as she plonked her iron down at our lodgings. My new faith was starting to wind people up.

I felt so awful that I booked an appointment at the vicarage.

'What's happening to me?' I asked the kindly vicar, sitting in his warm study, cup of tea in hand. 'Everyone thinks I'm crazy. Am I going mad?'

The vicar smiled at me. 'Judy, there's nothing wrong with you at all. Trust me – it's the Holy Spirit working in you.' I hadn't reckoned with the Holy Spirit. I had no idea that he would help me through the hardest parts of life ahead. I knew nothing then of the great adventures he would lead me into – the freedom, the joy and the peace.

After I made my commitment, I spent sixteen very happy months as a member of St Paul's Church, getting to know the people there and experiencing the fullness of a growing relationship with God. It took my mum time to adjust to the new me. I was so concerned to live in a godly way that I probably seemed to have become quite dull. I cut out the things that had elements of temptation for me, such as a celebratory party at a friend's home in Wales because of a mixed sleepover afterwards. I hated saying no, but I knew I was right to avoid the pitfalls which would stop me growing in my faith. But at the same time, life seemed to have become exciting and challenging – whole areas of my experience were changing, shifting and developing, as if I were waking from a long, dark dream.

The next time I climbed Cleeve Hill, it was with a friend from church who took communion at the top with me. I felt such a different person from the one who had escaped up there from the hospital only six months before.

In the summer of 1983, I received a discretionary award to study at London Bible College (now London School of Theology) in Northwood, Middlesex. Later, I would discover that by leaving Cheltenham I had just missed the man I would later marry – he joined St Paul's only a few months after I moved away! Although our paths didn't cross then, looking back I can see how a loving God was already weaving the tapestry in our lives to bring us together. But not yet.

At this point I was even more enthusiastic about my new faith and wanted to know more about God – so much so that I considered missionary work overseas. But as the Bible course progressed, I became more interested in the pastoral side of things, and so after completing two years of study, I returned to nursing in a local hospital, and then in a Christian hospice.

I had kept in touch with friends at St Paul's, had worked in the parish for two weeks on summer assignment, and returned to visit on several occasions. One day I took my favourite walk up Cleeve Hill and felt a strong sensation that God was drawing me back to the area to use my new skills and training, perhaps in St Paul's in a local job.

So one evening in 1988, aged 29, I took the plunge and steadily drove back to Cheltenham in my replacement car – an old white Ford Escort estate I called Timothy – stacked high with everything I owned. I'd left the two-roomed ground floor flat that I had enjoyed sharing with a friend, and turned up, uninvited, on St. Paul's vicarage doorstep. The sympathetic vicar's wife took me in until I found a bedsit to rent in the city centre.

I was still single, and didn't feel optimistic – while I was in Cambridge, the ratio of guys to girls was said to be 3 to 1, and my Bible college was often nicknamed the London Bridal College. I wondered what was wrong with me. Why was I still single? It hardly seemed possible that I would meet my Mr Right in a small Anglican church in a downbeat area of town.

While I was having coffee after a service at St Paul's, I noticed a guy I recognized – he had been introduced to me at a wedding four years earlier. The vicar's wife had beckoned me to one side at the start of the reception. 'Judy, there's someone I want you to meet – he's Russell, the man I've been telling you about, the one we're all praying for. You know, the one who's just joined the church.' She didn't labour the point but I knew she was talking about the man with all the issues I had heard about in prayer requests.

'Hi, I'm Judy,' I had said, sitting down tentatively next to Russell at the long table. 'Hi,' replied the stranger, glancing at me reticently for a moment, then quickly dropping his eyes. His short brown hair was flecked with red and the colour highlighted the freckles on his face.

When he stood to shake my hand he was 6 feet high, with a shy smile. He seemed reserved with me, but even at that first meeting I detected humour behind a gaunt and shy exterior. As we chatted, I found him quiet, but with a quality of focusing on me which was flattering and attractive. He was daunted by the crowd of people and left early, so reluctant to draw attention to himself that he left his unlabelled present in a corner of the room.

I had known at that wedding there was a definite connection between us, some mutual but unspoken acknowledgement, which I thought about after we said goodbye. But now here he was again, drinking coffee with me at the back of church four years later. I glanced at the fingers of his left hand, pleased that he wasn't wearing a wedding ring. That made me smile into my coffee cup.

Again there was some kind of mutual acknowledgement between us, an almost imperceptible sense of somehow being together. That seems strange considering that it would be nine years from our first meeting until our marriage.

3

RUSS

As I got to know him, I gradually learnt the full story of Russell's involvement at St Paul's Church. He had joined after admitting to himself that he needed Christ in his life. In the many long conversations we had in those early months, he told me about his chequered past.

Russell was born in Liverpool, where his parents met at university. He was the middle of three children, sandwiched between Philip and his younger sister, Eira. His parents had separated when Russell was very young, and his father was working as an architect in Saudi Arabia. Before the separation it was a hard life for his mother Sybil, who was a well-educated woman. She moved back to England and took the children to live with her mother in a detached 1930s house in St Albans.

One advantage of his father working overseas was that Russell developed a deep appreciation and understanding of the world. His mother and grandmother did an expert job in bringing up the three children, although Russell didn't then have any awareness of a loving God overseeing his life. Two definite marks of his character were an enquiring mind and impish sense of humour, and both remained deeply ingrained through all but the most challenging times. A teacher's comment from primary school referred to Russell having aptitude but often wasting it. He was able to keep a lot of pain inside, though. I was shocked to hear about the cruelty he had suffered from a housekeeper who had looked after him in Saudi Arabia while his father was at work. Russell didn't tell me the details, but the emotional scars never left him.

When he was in his mid teens his life took a downward turn and around this time his mother announced her remarriage, and he began to rebel in earnest. Things became tumultuous, especially after the death of his father in a motorcycle accident aged only 41. By then Russell was 16.

Although he had an excellent brain, he said he'd squandered much of his ability, especially at school. At 17 he reluctantly accepted a place at Surrey University, encouraged by his mother, where, on top of drinking excessively, he tried a variety of drugs. He said he often took drugs to ease his shyness and lack of self-esteem – but also for pure experimentation. There were occasional out-of-body experiences under the influence and Russell would smoke rather than inject heroin as he had a phobia of needles. He shared with me how his life at university had been desolate.

As Russell described this phase of his life I began to realize what a strong-willed character he must be. Each time he opened up and shared parts of his story with me on our walks on Cleeve Hill and meals together, I understood him better – although I was often shocked and strangely compelled by what I heard.

Russell had dropped out of university after one year and become interested in a sect that practised mind control. Back in his home town of St Albans, he attended weekend events with the sect and endeavoured to convince his mother and brother to follow suit. The effects of this mind control included a temporary increase in self-confidence and an outward appearance of being strong. Once he fearlessly challenged a crowd of Hell's Angels to a game of snooker in a pub and beat every one of them. During these months he was afraid of nothing, but gradually he came to see that the cult had no real answer to life's big questions, and that their lifestyle could even be seriously dangerous.

Russell continued smoking heroin, funding his drug habit from an inheritance he'd received. At this time he was sharing a house which he said resembled a squat; at one point he counted 100 dirty milk bottles in the kitchen. He took on some casual work but was unreliable, and he ploughed a lot of time, money and energy into renovating an old bus with a friend, a project that eventually came to nothing. While living this independent life in his early twenties, he rarely visited home, so his family didn't realize the severity of his situation. His brother, Phil, was becoming increasingly concerned though, and eventually suggested that Russell move to Cheltenham to live near him. Russell agreed, finding Phil to be accepting and non-judgemental.

Eventually Russell rented a room in the St Paul's area, near to his brother. He told me that looking back he was learning the truth of the verse in Proverbs 17:17, 'A friend loves at all times, and a brother is born for adversity.'

Despite Phil's support, Russell continued with his alcohol and heroin abuse and described his early weeks in Cheltenham to me as 'wretched'. He once pointed out a park bench where he had spent the odd night, sleeping off the effects of heroin. His past was so completely different from mine, and I struggled to connect with his memories, however hard I tried. I often thought of the old proverb which goes something like this: 'We cannot truly understand another person until we have walked a mile in their shoes.'

Alone in his little rented room, Russell took the drastic decision to come off drugs. He spent two weeks in agony, vomiting and sweating as he withdrew from heroin. Russell was not prone to exaggerate and I believed him when he told me that he came close to death over those two weeks. In desperation, at his lowest point, Russell dragged himself to the top of my favourite place on Cleeve Hill, with its breathtaking views over Cheltenham. This is what he told me.

> For me that was the clear moment when I turned my life over to God. And it was a wretched, miserable life. I was 22, and faced up to the truth – I was one of life's takers, not a giver. I wasn't contributing anything worthwhile to society. For a few years I'd been searching for meaning and direction in my life, but Christianity was never on my agenda. I'd looked in lots of wrong directions, but on the top of the hill – you know how breathtaking the views are, Judy, that day I could see as far as the Black Mountains – I just cried out in my pain, 'God, if you are there, help me!'
>
> Immediately a question popped into my mind. 'Why don't you become a Christian?'
>
> I felt totally broken, and actually sensed the presence of God for the first time. I admitted I'd wasted the life I'd been given, and right there I gave him the whole mess, telling God I wanted to make something worthwhile of my life. I didn't understand all the ins and outs of Jesus' death on the cross in a personal way, I just felt God was real and could be trusted. Straight away I knew I'd been forgiven, and from that moment the changes in my life proved it. Not long afterwards I began to identify with

John Newton, who years before me felt the same and knew he didn't deserve párdon. His hymn, 'Amazing Grace' struck a massive chord with me.

When I got back to my room, I started to read my grandmother's enormous Bible – like the ones that used to sit on lecterns in old churches. While I was actually reading it, my concentration was interrupted by a knock at the door. It was Marc, a member of the local church, inviting me to hear Billy Graham the next Sunday in Bristol. I'd never heard of Billy Graham and when Marc said he would be talking about Jesus Christ, I agreed to go right away.

Marc was totally flabbergasted – he wasn't used to such a positive reaction in the parish in those days! I had already begun to see that this coincidence of timing was God's hand reaching out to me.

Marc left me with a copy of the booklet *Journey into Life* by Norman Warren which explained the basics of Christianity and how to live and grow as a Christian. It also stressed the importance of prayer, reading the Bible and meeting with others who know Christ.

I went along on that Saturday, 15 May 1984, and after Billy Graham spoke, he invited anyone who wanted to make a commitment to come to the front of the stadium. I went forward. From that moment, and after my experience on the hill, I knew beyond a shadow of doubt that my name had been written in the Book of Life. Right then I chose to stand with everyone who wanted to turn their lives around and start again with Christ.

Russell explained to me that when he stepped forward at the Billy Graham event, he had entered into a commitment with God, fully adopted into God's family and under his protection.

I chose to trust in the One I couldn't see with my eyes, but who felt closer than my deepest thought. I later understood how Jesus' death and resurrection put me right with God. Jesus had taken the weight of my sins and made a way through to God for me. I didn't understand any of that in the stadium, but right away I knew Jesus was real and I could trust him.

The assurance of forgiveness affected Russell deeply, and he said to me later, 'I came from a background of degradation and sin. I had very little in the way of possessions and money – nothing to lose and everything to gain. The offer of new life in Christ and forgiveness of sins was too good to miss.'

It amused me to hear how his logical mind and determination were immediately obvious on the return coach journey from the Billy Graham event: 'I asked where the vicar was on the bus. When I was introduced, I told him I'd need to come and talk with him straight away. We had a long series of meetings, and although my mental ability was still affected by the after-effects of drugs and alcohol, the vicar said I stretched his knowledge to the hilt.'

Russell's understanding and powers of reasoning were obvious. From that point it was clear to everyone that he had a very keen mind which was being sharpened and focused by the work of the Holy Spirit in his heart.

It wasn't long after that momentous time that Russell and I sat together as guests at the same wedding.

In the early days after Russell's conversion, two members of St Paul's Church, Mike and Richard began to call on him regularly to offer support.

Mike told me

During our first visit, we prayed that Jesus would speak to Russell through our time together. At that time he was a young guy at very low ebb, living alone, with only a few possessions. He asked us in and we sat in the fairly shabby front room. He seemed to welcome our visit, and I wondered if he was just glad to see any visitors at all. He seemed bewildered, exhausted, like someone who has reached the end of his own resources and has nothing left to offer. But I guess he must have seen something affirming in our attitude – two blokes who had invaded his last refuge – because he asked us to visit again. So we did. Each time we went, Russell had more questions – he ~~literally~~ bombarded us with NO! them! It was obvious how much he was thinking. In the UK in the 1980s many people were questioning the motives of anyone who talked about Jesus Christ or the renewing work of the Holy Spirit. Some Christians were even being accused of being 'in a sect', rather than a 'normal' Christian. I sensed that Russell needed to test us before he could put any confidence in us as a pair – Richard, the keen young student and me, his 40-year-old sidekick.

Over the years that followed, I watched Russell grow as a Christian, and in the words of his stepfather, there had been 'a total transformation'.

Russell felt and believed that by facing up to his own wretched state, he had allowed God to begin restoring 'the years the locusts have eaten' (Joel 2:25). He met regularly with other Christians informally and at church. As Russell had no church background, he sometimes found the services confusing, especially the structured Anglican liturgy, and unfathomable service books. But nothing diminished his determination to grow spiritually among this group of Christians, who he said he found caring and supportive. Through the vicar, and with the help of many others, Russell said he began to absorb the teaching of Jesus Christ and come to know him better personally. He would say, 'It was Jesus who transformed my life, Judy.'

An immediate effect of his conversion was that he resolved to put something back into society to compensate for what he had taken out. He wrote to me

> Before I was a Christian, I was happy to be unemployed, but after my conversion I felt it was right to look for a job. . . . I contacted the Cheltenham volunteer bureau to offer my services. Sometimes in the early days I was offered lunch by the person whose lawn I mowed and that would be my only meal for one or two days. I really struggled to break the pattern of spending my dole money on drink instead of food, and at first I would turn up slightly the worse for drink at evening Bible study meetings and no one even seemed to notice.

I realized the church group probably did know what was going on but turned a blind eye, as they appreciated him as an individual and recognized that Jesus came to help the sick rather than the healthy.

An elderly lady who was the mother of a member of St Paul's offered Russell a bedsit instead of his single room. The new arrangement worked very well, even though he came home from his new paid job at a mushroom farm with a pungent smell on his clothes. She just accepted Russell as he was and became another link in the process of helping to rebuild his self-esteem.

He also told me that at around this time he became aware of having a special spiritual gift which gave him great encouragement. He would read a piece from the gospels before going to sleep at night, and then dream vividly that he was present at the scene described in his reading. For example, on the night he read about Jesus' miraculous healing of the paralyzed man, he dreamt of being part of the very crowd, witnessing Jesus and his works as they happened.

But then he seemed to fall back into his old ways again. He never said whether he had reverted to drinking or simply neglected his new faith, but the gift left and never returned. 'I learnt a big lesson from that, and it was a turning point – afterwards, my mind was firmly set on following Christ with no going back.'

It was at that time that he was offered paid work as a sort of 'Man Friday' to the woman whose husband ran the mushroom farm where Russell had been working, on the lower slopes of Cleeve Hill. She was recovering from a spell in hospital and needed help. There was pay and free accommodation with the job, and he knew this was his chance of financial independence. He told me the job had removed him from the potentially harmful influence of people from his old life before conversion. 'But the application form posed a big problem,' Russell said. He went on

> There was the usual question, 'Do you have a criminal record?' And I did have a minor offence; nothing serious enough to make headlines, but it was still an offence. I thought that most people would just keep quiet about it, and after thinking it through I decided to do just that. I was offered the job but after accepting it I felt so bad that I went to my employer and came clean. I just couldn't go on living with the lie. God didn't give up on me, my employer didn't either, and I kept the job!

The job fulfilled him; he threw himself into it vigorously and willingly, and came to love his own little flat at the far end of the enormous rambling house. He told me about the tremendous battles as his drug-damaged mind fought with the darkness which often enveloped him: 'But all the time I could feel that my mind and body were being restored after the hammering they'd taken, and I knew healing all the effects would be a really gradual process.'

People encouraged him to take up his old hobby of playing in a brass band. He had played the trumpet, and now decided in favour of the cornet, joining the Winchcombe town band, a group which proved to be made up of kind and accepting people. Russell said, 'I was filling up my spare time with good things, because I knew that would leave less opportunity for my old habits. I'd got hold of a bike and I would hurtle over Cleeve Hill to band practice in Winchcombe, come rain or shine.'

Before long, Russell's colleague, Peter, joined him in the flat. Peter told me

It would be wrong to say we agreed on everything; in fact, it was quite the opposite. But I think we grew to understand each other's viewpoint as time went on, and we enjoyed a good bachelor-pad relationship. Often we giggled like schoolboys, laughing at the most stupid things. I know the Deakins's thought very highly of him. They saw Russell as their own Jeeves, and always said how diligently he worked on the farm. And there was the tennis – we were both fiercely competitive players, and the walk home back up the hill was a long one for whichever one of us lost.'

Russell struck up a close relationship with Giles, the youngest son of Mike, who had met with him in the early days. Mike says

Russell and Giles had a kind of second childhood together. I watched them play bat and ball in the back garden, and they sometimes camped on the hill and even went potholing. I was a bit bothered by Russell's adventurous risk-taking, but it worked out OK in the end.

Mike had sensed that the extreme danger posed less of a threat to him in those days than relating to people did! I remembered hearing how fed up he was that a whole day's instruction was needed before he took a parachute jump. He just wanted to leap straight out of the plane.

Mike's story reminded me of a tale Russell's mother's told me about a family holiday on Exmoor. She was busy putting up the tent when the young Russell calmly announced that he'd found a good place to relieve himself. She found him between two high rocks, with one foot on top of each rock and a sheer drop in between!

In those early days, Mike knew Russell was finding his feet in many areas of life, and that throughout he took Jesus seriously and had a real awareness of having been rescued. He sought to put right any wrongs that were outstanding in his life, including writing to his stepfather to ask forgiveness for his rebellious youth.

During the summer of 1984, a friend of mine from London Bible College was doing some practical training in St Paul's Church. Russell said he felt privileged to spend an hour or two daily with him, sitting under the apple tree in the vicarage garden, studying the book of Romans. I always knew that the squashed dead fly he insisted on keeping in the pages of chapter 6 of Romans was a memory of this time, but it was much later that I understood its symbolism. Russell knew that as a Christian he was 'dead to sin', and the fly was his personal reminder of this!

4

JUDY

My own past had been a lot less dramatic than Russell's, but I had followed a winding road to the point where we eventually met.

I have always enjoyed acting and my earliest 'performance' was in *Love from Judy*, in which my mum played the lead role while she was four and a half months pregnant with me. That's how I came to be named Judy, and I have been forever thankful that she didn't conceive me in her earlier roles of Tuptim, Buttercup or Cerubino.

When I was 9, I watched my mother perform as Eliza in *My Fair Lady* and clapped so hard I thought my palms would bleed. I clutched my dad's hand and listened to my mother hold the audience captive with her beautiful soprano voice. Afterwards, we weaved along the theatre corridor to her room, stepping over bouquets and bouquets of flowers, all for her. Next morning at home, the hall was so crammed with flowers that I couldn't walk through them.

My parents described me as a tactile, trusting – almost gullible – and compassionate child, often trying to protect wildlife, and loving affection. I only remember telling three lies as a child – one after I had climbed out of my bedroom window at 5.30 a.m. to meet my friend, Kaye, who lived down the road; we sat in her shed eating baked beans and drawing up stringent rules for our '259 Club'. When Mum pointed out the mud marks on my windowsill and demanded to know the truth, I claimed to know nothing.

After leaving school in 1977, I worked on a Kibbutz in Israel for several months. At that time, gap years weren't particularly common but my nursing training didn't start until the next year and I wanted adventure. Camp America sounded too much like a place for rich kids, whereas I was fascinated to experience the communal living and sharing in a Kibbutz!

The first Kibbutz I worked in was near the Golan Heights; a dangerous time in a dangerous place – gunmen shot anything that moved after the 6 p.m. curfew. One evening I very foolishly took a late hike on the mountain and survived. It must have been the breath-taking walk down the hill that attracted me – or perhaps the friendly Israeli I walked with.

I even boarded the plane home in tears after my three-and-a-half month stay, considering postponing my flight because I couldn't bear to leave one Polish guy behind. I was always searching for 'The One' and as soon as I realized a boyfriend was not him, I moved on.

For me, it was a time of enlightenment and excitement. At one party for the volunteers, I was shocked to watch two drunk girls almost fall into the open fire. I hitched lifts with army guys, quite usual for us volunteers back then, and slept beside the Sea of Galilee. I climbed Mount Sinai at 2 a.m. to watch the sunrise, after the most uncomfortable night of my life trying to sleep on the rocks because I wasn't prepared to pay £2 to sleep in St Katherine's Monastery.

We picked apples and worked night shifts in a bottle factory, inhaling plastic fumes as we clipped the edges from bottle tops. In the apple processing plant I took my breaks with an elderly Israeli and sipped strong Turkish coffee. I did refuse to work in a chicken house where I was told to hold four chickens at a time and hurl them into a lorry. As a youngster I had written to the Minister of Agriculture about animal cruelty.

I started smoking in Israel, partly because the Israelis gave us free cigarettes every Friday and after several weeks of giving mine away, I decided to try one; and partly because smoking cigarettes was what everybody did while we stood around chatting. I was more than a social smoker; I genuinely enjoyed a cigarette and always feared I wouldn't be able to stop at one. It wasn't until five years later when I denied smoking on a form for my Bible college that I declared to myself and God that the cigarette I was smoking would be my last. And it was.

I did see a certain amount of sharing among the people of the Kibbutz – although some residents still had their own places – but I didn't like to see children sleeping away from their parents in the children's house. I loved cleaning the communal dining room floor by chucking water from a bucket and guiding it down the stairs with a broom. Even more I loved riding on a lorry at 5.30 a.m., often wearing the sought-after blue cotton shirt and trousers from the clothes bank. I would then spend a couple of hours apple picking, returning to an enormous breakfast of whole cucumbers, cinnamon porridge and cream cheese. No wonder my mum said I looked like a navvy when I came home.

I also stayed in a second Kibbutz nearer to Jerusalem and by the sea. I loved the element of risk in my life at that time, feeling the excitement and challenge similar to when I used to see if my moped could just reach my destination without my petrol totally running out on me. My experience in Israel introduced me to people who didn't know where they were going; I knew I was privileged to have my nursing training to go to. Although I wasn't following God wholeheartedly, I knew he was there and couldn't envisage denying him. I had an idea there was so much more to being a Christian, but I didn't want that – yet.

I began my RGN nurse training at Addenbrooke's Hospital, Cambridge, in 1978. Now a restaurant and student lodgings, the old Addenbrooke's I lived in had bars at the windows and matrons in starched caps who expelled any student nurses caught with a fiancé staying the night.

My reason for choosing nursing as a career was based on a vague idea I had of helping people in Africa. I think I probably chose Cambridge as I heard the city had a ratio of three guys to one girl – so maybe this was where I would meet my Mr Right.

My favourite wards were cancer and neurology. In those days, survival rates for cancer were far lower than they are now, and I learnt that many patients on the cancer ward appreciated the life they had left so much more than the young, frustrated guys with fractured legs on other wards. On the cancer ward I felt I could help make a difference. The ward sister really cared, and I never minded staying long over my time.

Very early on I saw my first patient die, and my eyes instinctively looked up to the window. I had an idea that she had faith, and I felt certain that now her spirit was free. I asked a middle-aged man in a side room opposite if he would like me to read to him from the Bible.

'Please do!' he begged, and when I had finished he said, 'Do you know, I haven't heard the Bible since I was a boy.' He seemed truly moved.

The neurology team was a pleasure to work with and I liked the layout and atmosphere there; it was less austere and clinical than other wards. The study of the brain fascinated me, and it was there I learnt to talk to the patients even though it appeared they could not hear. The realization dawned that I was always more drawn to aspects of nursing that involved patients' psychological needs.

After training I was disappointed not to be placed on either of my favourite wards but on the leukaemic ward, the busiest ward in the new hospital. My feet hardly touched the ground, but I was always happier when we had less beds and I felt I could care properly for the patients. In the early mornings I would sit writing reports and eating a piece of hot buttered toast, watching the sun lifting its head outside the window. I often floated around with an open white gown over my uniform, thinking it was more homely – one patient woke with a start and thought he had seen an angel, which was flattering!

In those days the reality of people's conditions didn't really hit me and I would chat away to them about where I was going on holiday, not quite connecting with what was really going on for them.

My secondment in psychiatry taught me a great deal about not taking offence at rudeness. After I encouraged one woman to wash her own face she told me I was 'Too f***ing lazy to do anything'. But I did have a great group of nursing friends and we threw ourselves into the parties, once swimming in the fellows' private pool, and getting out to discover our clothes had been hidden. Again I met many guys of various nationalities during my training – but no Mr Right.

In January 1982 I made the conscious decision to move from Cambridge to be out of my comfort zone so I would have no more excuse to avoid following Christ.

I chose Cheltenham, partly because Dad and I thought the Cotswolds were pretty. Dad drove me to my job interview and we enjoyed breakfast at the Queen's Hotel, on the Promenade, where I relished the individual little jars of marmalade.

In the new job I enjoyed working in a much smaller hospital. Although I missed the caring aspect of nursing, I really enjoyed teaching young mums. However, when I received an emergency call from my dad to say my grandmother was dying and that they needed me, I requested time off knowing staff cover was available. I was refused leave, and was told to choose between my family and my profession. I chose my family . . . and somehow kept my job.

It was during this time that I became a Christian and everything in my life began to change. That included my decision to stop leading guys on. It was a tough decision, especially as everyone else except me seemed to have a boyfriend.

In the summer of 1983 I had received the discretionary award to study at London Bible College. I absolutely loved the college, loved the variety of people – there were over twenty nationalities represented – loved the lectures, the library, and the friendships. I especially enjoyed sketchboard preaching in Leicester Square. At this time I felt the seeds of a yearning to speak to large groups of people, and to pray for individuals. A picture formed in my mind of speaking to hundreds of people from a balcony.

I felt sure God had said I would marry, but I had no idea when. The fear crossed my mind that I might be 80 before it happened! I had been dating a fellow student who had another year left to study, and we were wondering if we had a future together. He became less sure, and the stress of the relationship led to me being signed off work with stress tension, and my wise doctor advising me to sort out the relationship one way or another.

The time now seemed right to find a nursing job close to college. After turning down a position at the prestigious Mount Vernon cancer unit, I felt it was right to hold out for a job at the local cottage hospital, which I had applied for but received no reply. So I returned to stay with my parents without a job, and having to explain to people why I had turned down a really good one. It was all because I sensed God was guiding me to wait.

It turned out that my job application had been lost in a rarely used mailbox at the cottage hospital, and once they found it, I was offered an interview and job soon afterwards. I loved caring for the patients at Northwood, Pinner and District Hospital, and enjoyed the variety and homeliness there. As their only full-time staff nurse, I was involved in the managerial side, and the low-key setting suited me perfectly.

A couple of years later, I read in the church notice sheet of a Christian hospice and continuing care unit that was opening in Chorleywood, Hertfordshire. My interest was aroused straight away – especially as the cottage hospital had been urging me to take a course in research, which didn't interest me in the slightest. So I decided to leave.

I settled easily into Thorpedale as the junior sister, although as a charity my wages couldn't be guaranteed. At the time I had no mortgage and felt very strongly that the job was God's idea and a perfect opportunity to use my nursing qualifications and care for people in a Christian setting. For the first time I would be able to put my Bible training to use and speak freely about my faith. Thorpedale was a very special place, where we experienced many people putting their trust in Christ before they died. To me it seemed that he was walking around the hospice and whispering his presence.

Sadly, Thorpedale had to close after a few years. A minister described us as a broken fruit bowl, with the implication that we, the staff, would be spread out but still very much part of the ongoing work that God had been doing there.

In 1988, after a short career diversion into a finance company, I took a job at the Sue Ryder hospice in Cheltenham. It was a privilege to nurse there and I saw many examples of God's power at work – often most evident in my difficult times. As a single woman, at first I felt lonely and different, as well as misunderstood because of my faith. But God gave me amazing times, such as with a woman who was constantly begging me to pray on her behalf. One morning I swapped shifts and was attending another woman in the next room who had only been admitted the night before. Her admission details gave her religion as 'Christian'. She told me that an unusual thing had happened to her at 3 o'clock that morning. She had woken and felt a strong urge to pray for the woman in the next room. I gasped to myself as I knew (which this patient didn't) that the woman she spoke of had been seeking God – and also that she had died that morning at 3 a.m.

5

ROMANCE

It was one evening in October 1988 when I returned to Cheltenham with a carload of possessions. In no time at all I was renting a bedsit and very soon was receiving regular visits from the mushroom grower on a bicycle! Somehow I always seemed to be looking down from the window of my townhouse bedsit when his bicycle bell jingled. Once, our future best man arrived to call on me at the same moment. In the early days Russell was hesitant with people, and he told me later that at that time he looked up to me. We had fun together, and were soon meeting for a pizza, walking up the hill or spending time studying the Bible, always learning more about God and sensing his presence with us.

Each time I visited his flat I couldn't help noticing that the main room was in desperate need of a coat of paint. One Sunday as we walked past some buildings I asked him, 'Which of those do you prefer – the restored or the dilapidated one?'

'The restored one, definitely.'

'Then why don't you paint your room?' I laughed.

And that's what he did.

Russell had saved enough for a red Vauxhall Cavalier, deliberately choosing a four-seater so he could drive elderly people to church services. He loved to be useful and felt he had so much to give. We once passed each other at a bend in the road, both sensing something significant in that crossing of our paths.

When I left his flat, Russell would cheerily wave goodbye as I reached the lowest step of his staircase, leaving me to brave the walk to the car on my own, with a fear of the dark to contend with. One day Mrs Deakin, the farmer's wife, rebuked him for this and I never had to walk to the car alone again. His naivety about dating and relationships was balanced by a growing maturity and wisdom in other areas. I found him loyal and diligent with a desire to serve and know God with all his being. That was very attractive to me – he was a man with purpose who was never afraid to be known as a Christian, valuing fun and friendship while putting God's will for his life above his own.

Sometimes we would deliver church service pamphlets together in the council area of St Paul's, and I would occasionally tell Russell off for clambering over the walls between houses. In many ways he was still locked in his own world. Once, as we were walking down a side street beside the park when he was particularly quiet, I asked if he was all right. He couldn't reply – he found the focus on him was too overwhelming. Later he explained that during those months God was gradually healing him, and that during his bleakest times his mind was resting while his body carried out the mundane, undemanding aspects of his job. Certain things he did really upset me – he would slip away from an evening meeting without saying goodbye to anyone, even me, and I felt cut off from his private inner world.

* hope this should be dual! Have you ever tried to jar 2 elderly blind people into the back of a 2 door car? From personal experience, DON'T! :)

My feelings for Russ (as I had come to call him) were growing stronger. But for the first time ever, and although we very much enjoyed being together, we each decided, independently, to cool things down. We agreed that if our relationship was to develop romantically, it would have to be clearly 'God-led' and not 'us-led'. I knew the folly of trying to work things out, because I had made such a mess of trying to manipulate relationships in the past. I needed assurance that it was God drawing us together, but had no idea how or if this would happen.

An opportunity arose for me to go to Uganda for two and a half months in 1990. I was profoundly affected by that trip. The African people love people to stand and share their story, and I did this in a prison. I was shocked to learn that some of the prisoners had been jailed for stealing nothing more than a loaf of bread. But I felt very much at home in the African environment and my passion for speaking grew stronger while I was there.

One afternoon I asked God to talk to me as I took a walk. Before my trip I had been in the habit of bombarding Russ with my ideas of moving to Oxford to train in health visiting, or up north for some other job. Now, as I walked, my attention was caught by a butterfly flitting here and there, and I sensed God was using this image to show me that I was behaving like that butterfly. The words came into my head: 'I want you to stay in Cheltenham and I will bring things to you.' Briefly Russ came into my mind, but I didn't dwell on the possible significance at the time. I sensed God begin to impress on me to leave the choice of a partner to him. In fact, I was actually becoming very fond of an African evangelist and he and I had a tear-jerking goodbye as he stood on the airport balcony and I sobbed into my hanky.

Soon after I returned home from my Uganda trip, I put a deposit down on a little house in Cheltenham opposite the church. There was a delightful miniature willow tree in the garden, and the building nestled amongst rows of little Victorian terraces, in varying stages of upkeep. Russ paid me regular visits; he was now playing the cornet in the police band and my new house just happened to lie on his route home! I vividly remember seeing his traditional police helmet appearing through the glass panel in the front door. One autumn evening I firmly told him that I had given my heart to my African friend. As I spoke the words I finally realized the truth of my growing feelings for Russ. As he left, both of us felt a great weight had lodged in the pit of our beings. He rang me an hour later and we agreed to continue our friendship. Russ had the overwhelming sense that it would be wrong not to go on seeing me. Soon afterwards I was delighted to hear that my African friend had met and married a woman from New Zealand, fulfilment indeed of a prophecy that he would marry a white person.

Russ often whisked me up Cleeve Hill to enjoy our favourite views and one evening we even gazed in wonder at the Northern Lights. It was after one of these walks that Russ and I sat in my lounge and first discussed whether we should be praying about a possible future together. For the next nine months we made it a matter of serious prayer and Bible study before it became clear that God was drawing us together. It was almost as though the pieces of a jigsaw puzzle were gradually forming into a whole and complete picture. I remember going out for tea one summer's day near Ross-on-Wye. We took the last table but both felt it was the best place in the tearoom; we later joked that our marriage was like that – we left it late, but came to know that we had made the best choice.

One warm summer evening, with the scent of cow parsley lingering in the air, we climbed Cleeve Hill. I was calling it a 'holy hill' in my journal because it was the exact spot where Russ had cried out to God in desperation eight years previously. We had just come from an uplifting weekly group Bible study at the newly built vicarage. Our hearts were full and we both knew that this was a special moment. Beneath my summer top my stomach fluttered. I knew Russ was about to propose and I felt excited and nervous all at the same time.

We sat down at the holy spot and there Russ asked me to be his wife. I said yes immediately. Then we prayed and walked downhill, hand in hand.

'Look, Judy. Glow-worms!' Russ said.

I looked and, sure enough, there they were, shimmering, and we both knew without a shadow of doubt that God was with us and would be in our future marriage. As I approached my door, I noticed two pieces of confetti on the doorstep – a crown and a heart. I looked around at the other doors but they had none; further confirmation within my heart that God, who is described as the King of kings, was present in our plans.

Although I knew God had been at work in both our lives, and that our engagement was God's timing, I wasn't so sure about the day we planned to announce our news to my family. We inadvertently chose the day of the Grand Prix to drive past Silverstone, and I became more and more frantic as the delay got longer. But when we eventually arrived at my parents' house, they were delighted and cracked open the champagne. Dad joked about our first visit, five months previously, 'They didn't give us much warning, but I liked Russ right away. He helped me put up the Christmas decorations!' And Mum loved him too – I think partly because of the duster he bought for her that first Christmas. He made her laugh and that counted for a lot with my mum.

Russ avoided the champagne as he had become teetotal seven years earlier, and I was very grateful to my parents – both social drinkers – for not questioning his abstinence then or later. They totally accepted him. Russ didn't touch a drop of alcohol for the rest of his life, and I never worried that he would. I believe God gave me that confidence and assurance; as his stepfather had said, Russ was totally transformed. I valued Russ as a man of integrity and substance – and was thrilled to find he no longer looked 'up' but 'across' to me.

He never made any attempt to conceal his past; it just didn't come up in most social situations. He had given his testimony a few times in our own church, but he knew he was still being healed and didn't want to dwell on the past and its dark associations. 'It's still too close, Judy,' he would say. 'I need time and space to consolidate what God's doing in my life first, before I talk about it.'

He had been very discouraged by one episode. He'd shared his testimony at a nearby church and a visitor had approached him afterwards saying, 'Oh, you're the one with the history of drugs!' He had just bared his soul and that incident hurt him deeply. It also made him realize he needed to be stronger before he could handle that kind of comment. So he stayed within his own church and instead, wrote some articles for the magazine based on the biblical prophet Jeremiah who had faced conflicts raging within and around him. Russ said he could identify with the relationship Jeremiah had with God that enabled him to withstand anguish and despair.

During this time, Russ always needed a lot of rest and my sister-in-law, Jackie, once remarked, 'Russ has got it sorted – I've always thought it's rather a good idea, to spend time recumbent!'

Two years before our marriage, Russ had bought a house with his friend Nick in a tough area of our parish where Nick felt he could convey Christ's love to the local kids. Despite the fact that they had excrement posted through the letterbox and experienced constant harassment, Russ never questioned Nick's decision. 'Nick went on to train as an officer in the Church Army,' said Russ, 'and I married Judy. I'm not sure which was the more daring venture!'

6

SEVEN YEARS OF MARRIAGE

We were married on 24 April 1993. Russ had been consistent in reading his Bible every day, and on the morning of our wedding his daily reading happened to be from Psalm 19: 'In the heavens he has pitched a tent for the sun, which is like a bridegroom coming forth from his pavilion, like a champion rejoicing to run his course'(vv. 4b,5a).

Although he was still shy, Russ stood under the Norman Arch at my childhood church, All Hallows, Wellingborough and personally greeted over two hundred guests. I was so proud of him, so proud to become his wife, and the service was like a fairy tale.

We walked out to the rousing sound of a solo trumpeter playing the 'Prince of Denmark's March', and as we stood in the west doorway for photos, I felt something being pressed into my hand by a lady in the crowd; it was a black cat charm. I wrestled with the desire not to cause offence, but had the spiritual conviction that it was wrong to accept any lucky charm and politely refused it. We were trusting God alone for our future.

On our honeymoon we toured for 2,000 miles around Scotland. We delighted in keeping the destination a secret. I have wonderful memories of sitting next to my new husband, hurtling down leafy lanes in our red Cavalier to arrive on time for a wonderful supper at a hotel or cosy bed and breakfast. We devoured enormous langoustines on the loch and our very own Scottish piper entertained us; we spent an hour or more surveying Loch Ness, hoping to spot the monster.

One day while walking in the mountains, we got separated and each independently had the sensation that the other had died. I found myself praying and reciting Psalm 23:4: 'Even though I walk through the valley of the shadow of death, I will fear no evil, for you are with me; your rod and your staff, they comfort me.' We were soon reunited, and decided to cut our walk short.

The rest of our honeymoon passed gloriously. We climbed Ben Nevis – the easy route – sat on our cagoules and slid down from the summit, skimming over the snow. Later in the week we made a journey to view the Old Man of Stour, a large rock rising through the sea several hundred metres from the land. As my newly acquired, high-spirited husband disappeared over the cliff edge to get a closer look, I told God I was not going to spend my married life worrying about him! So I took a walk in the opposite direction, and was thoroughly relieved when he reappeared. In time I would come to see his recklessness mellow, but he always maintained an appreciation and wonder for the natural world, something which I have learnt from him.

As with most honeymoons, ours had its first tiff. I made a sudden exit from the car on our way up a hill after the disagreement, and we later vowed to resolve issues right away, and never to let the sun go down on our anger. We tried to be 'other-centred' and to make an effort to understand the needs of our individual temperaments.

Crucially, we actively sought Christ's support in our marriage. He never let us down.

During the seven years of very happy marriage that followed, Russ grew stronger and steadier all the time. He was working hard and the farm had implemented two of his innovative ideas, which led to a substantial increase in their profit. Russ had already told me how he had sat on a tree stump next to Pittville Lake and prayed for God to move him on to a new and bigger challenge. I felt this was one of those significant prayers of faith which expected a response.

Russ began a home study course in computing, and afterwards applied to train in computer programming. The tutor phoned and asked him to consider his application carefully because it would be a demanding course and his present job was very different. After waiting one minute, with typical impetuousness Russ phoned the tutor straight back: 'I've given it tremendous consideration and I've decided to take the course!' He passed the course with flying colours. One evening our phone rang when we were finishing supper. It was a respected manager for Spirax Sarco. Russ had been rather despondent a few days earlier when he returned from yet another interview without being offered the job. 'I was close,' he said, 'but close isn't good enough.'

He was intrigued that the manager himself was on the phone. I heard him say, 'Yes, please. Thank you very much, sir.' He put the phone down and a look of wonder and appreciation came over his face.

'He wants to hire me, Judy. He wants to give me a job.'

This man had demonstrated his faith in Russ by hiring him. That was a special moment in our lives and Russ duly left the farm, the place he felt had been God's choice for that time. Although sometimes hard and frustrating, the farm had been a real stepping stone in his life.

Whenever I started negative murmurings, Russ would remind me that we had entered into what he called 'a time of blessing'. I could hardly get my head around our happiness together. I tried to protect myself from losing it, sometimes saying, 'You're not going to die on me, are you?' Many times in my insecurity I imagined the helmet of a real policeman appearing at the door, coming to tell me that Russ had had an accident.

Russell's impish humour and daring past often came to light in those days. At family get-togethers his brother, Phil, and sister, Eira, delighted in sharing stories of their youth. I heard about the time when both boys rolled Eira in a barrel down their very long garden, about Russ setting up a chemical experiment that ran the length of the school lab tables, jumping from one Bunsen burner to the next, and the time when their grandmother (who was totally oblivious to their escapades at the foot of the garden) heard an explosion and put it down to the weather at that time of year. Married life with Russ was equally unpredictable. When my brother, Nick, was visiting with my American sister-in-law, Jackie, and my niece and nephew, Laura and David, we took them to a Roman site near Cirencester. Suddenly Russ scrabbled around on the floor with his foot near one of the baths and bent down to uncover a Roman coin.

Jackie could hardly contain herself. 'So is it really a genuine coin, Russ? Do you think it's really worth something?'

He thought for a while and then calmly announced, 'About 50p. That's how much I paid for it in the gift shop when we came in!'

Russ was much more logical than me, and genuinely sought to understand my perspective on things. In time he came to know me very well, and I grew in understanding him. In our second year of marriage I conceived two babies and we were so upset when both miscarried early in pregnancy – we thought they were boys and named them both.

In 1995, to our total delight and joy, our first daughter, Rachel, was born. My parents loved to describe the day that we made a casual call to my mother from the phone box at the bottom of her road in Wellingborough, which was a two-hour drive from our house in Cheltenham. Mum assumed we were at home and was stunned only minutes later to answer the front door and find little Rachel smiling up at her all alone on the doorstep. 'Brian!' she called to my father. 'Well, Rachel's here!' I can still see Russ's laughing face as we stepped forward.

We moved house twice within a year, both within Bishops Cleeve, an overdeveloped village on the outskirts of Cheltenham. The second time was just a week before Lucy was born: Russ was under the weather at that time, and he spent much of her delivery flat on the labour room floor. As with Rachel, Lucy was a source of total delight to us. From early on her vitality and zest for life kept both her and us awake.

Russ was becoming increasingly at ease with people, and feeling more able to socialize. I was relieved because he had married into a very people-orientated family. On Christmas day at my parents' home a hundred or so would gather in the vast hall for carols round the piano. This was a baptism of fire for Russ, who was used to a quieter life. One Christmas afternoon he sneaked off to an empty room and managed to watch the whole of *Jurassic Park* in relative peace. His love of nature extended to the dinosaur era, sea life and outer space – I loved to fall asleep listening to his descriptions of the vast and awesome universe. He never tired of teaching me even the most basic astronomical facts.

Our happiness was absolute. On holiday we skinny-dipped, and in a secluded part of our garden we made love in the moonlight. We delighted in being together.

Russ loved our new Bovis cottage-style home and surprised me with his capabilities as a handyman. He had spoken of his love for DIY when we first married, but I had never seen any evidence of it. Now I realized that all he had previously lacked was inspiration. The new setting was perfect, and in no time at all Russ had designed and begun building a beautiful replica of our home as a doll's house for the girls. He furnished and decorated it just like the real thing, and little Rachel sat in the garage watching him work with her eyes full of wonder.

Lucy made Thursday evening trips to Sainsbury's with her daddy, returning with two Teletubby chocolates, one for her sister. On one of these trips, Russ looked over at his younger daughter in the supermarket and said, 'Your name is Lucy. And I'm your daddy!' Quick as a flash Lucy replied, 'Well done, Daddy!' patting his chest with her chubby little fingers. Russ was still laughing when they returned home! He was always so proud of his girls and loved telling friends about their progress. He loved pushing them in wheelbarrows or luggage trolleys, and lifting them onto his shoulders so they would peer in at me suddenly through the high kitchen window. To quote Russ's godfather, I had indeed married 'a bundle of irrepressible good fun'.

7

DIAGNOSIS

Friday, 23 June 2000 is the day my life changed for ever. For several weeks I had been waking to the sound of birdsong at 5.30 a.m. and slipping downstairs to pray. I sensed that it was God waking me, and I would sit in the middle of our white rug, repeatedly telling him of my submission to him and his purposes for my life.

In those early mornings I leafed through a favourite book of mine, *Risky Living*, by Jamie Buckingham, and thought about my years of trusting God prior to my marriage, when life had often seemed very hard. Those years of risky living had been a period of pain, but also of great joy as I walked hand in hand with God.

Looking back now it seems that during those days, Russ was encouraging me to grow in my own relationship with God. Even though we had no idea of the path ahead, I do think I was being prepared for when Russ would no longer be by my side. When domestic decisions came along, he encouraged me to shoulder them. I am sure that, patient as he was, I did exasperate him at times, as I found it hard to make many small decisions over issues such as which playgroup to book the girls into, and whether it was a good idea for Rachel to take ballet lessons.

Because Russ was such a strong character, in the weeks leading up to 23 June 2000 we didn't realize that his body was weakening. He had been tired in his previous job, but we put this down to a lack of stimulation. Now with an exciting new job as a senior programmer, he was quickly displaying a new vitality in his life. He had been taking on lots of new activities, including training as a reader at church – a lay ministerial role which involved him preaching, teaching, and taking on pastoral duties. We believed this was part of God's plan for him. He had also taken on the church end-of-year accounts, and it was still common for the mushroom farm to call on him, asking for his help with the Mr Mushroom programme he had devised for them years earlier.

He was including more and more personal testimony in his speaking, and devoting hours to preparation, yearning for more inspiration from the Holy Spirit. As well as all these things, he was working at being able to improvise on the cornet and we had been praying about all these concerns.

Russ really seemed to have more energy in his new job and although he had begun to suffer periodically from headaches at work, he made little mention of them at home. Nonetheless, I mentioned them to my optician, who invited him for an eye test. He thought Russ might be developing short-sightedness – and as a computer programmer, was entitled to regular eye checks.

It is always easier in hindsight to spot signs of illness; these often go unnoticed in the course of daily life. There was nothing that struck us as particularly serious – and headaches are not uncommon. All this coincided with a visit from our financial advisor, and at this point we discussed whether to take sickness insurance and decided against it. Around this time I insisted that we buy a new bed, as Russ had always found our double bed hard, and it was affecting his sleep pattern. His sleep had been erratic as long as I had known him, but we knew his difficulty in sleeping was making him tired and he frequently took a nap when he came home from work. We chose an enormous bed and I still wonder how we got it up the stairs! It was wonderfully soft, and the effect on Russ was immediate. He was so much more rested that he managed to devote two whole days to catching up with jobs around the house, and even surprised Rachel by collecting her at school pick-up time.

Despite sleeping better, it was not unusual for Russ to wake with his pyjama top soaked with sweat. A friend with chronic fatigue syndrome was having similar symptoms, and we did wonder whether Russ might have a mild form of the same condition. He never complained or took sick days, and as we were so preoccupied with our young children at home, we disregarded these signs. Because we were familiar with his behaviours, it wasn't easy to register that something was wrong. Russ had always needed rest even though he had tremendous physical and mental strength, so we saw no obvious signs of a life-threatening illness.

One morning someone complained they had a cold when we were leaving church and Russ quietly whispered in my ear, 'Crikey, if she felt like I do all the time, she wouldn't be moaning about a cold!' That comment shocked and surprised me.

I remember speaking on the phone to a good friend who had just returned from a funeral, and I found myself repeating his words, 'Marriage is in sickness and in health.' As I gazed out of my kitchen window, these words seemed to hold a depth and resonance for me,

almost as if I were declaring something deeply important and relevant, without knowing why.

As a mum with small children, I rarely had any time
to myself. On 21 June 2000, I took to the bathroom, one
hand clutching a copy of *A Testament of Devotion* by
Thomas R. Kelly, a Quaker missionary and scholar,
while I shaved my legs! I had reached the chapter about
suffering and read, 'An awful solemnity is upon the
earth, for the last vestige of earthly security is gone. It
has always been gone, and religion has always said so,
but we haven't believed it.'[1] These words struck me
forcibly, with their implication that we so often assume
everything is secure when, in fact, it is not.

When he had joined the company Spirax Sarco, Russ
had been given a medical check-up with an all-clear. We
decided to contact our doctor, and booked an appointment for the evening of 23 June 2000. The GP assessed
Russ's symptoms as non-specific, but thought it would
be wise to send him for a blood test.

On 24 June, the morning after seeing the doctor, Russ
drove to the financial advisor to finalize some details
before going on to have the blood test. Then he took the
car for a short service and drove the girls and me for a
swim at Tewkesbury. I remember noticing how well
Russ managed the children, giving me time to swim two
lengths. He had fun chasing the girls round the little
pool, and I was delighted to see he had more energy. We
came home singing in the car.

That same evening he was in the bath when the phone
rang. It was the doctor, asking if he could visit us immediately. I asked why, and he told me that Russ had a high
white cell count. As I had worked as a trained nurse for
many years, I understood what he meant and called
upstairs to say the doctor was coming. He just said,
'Right, I'll get out and come downstairs.'

Minutes later, I spotted the doctor approaching the house. The last time I had seen him was nine years before, when I worked at the Sue Ryder hospice; I had shown him around the wing. I don't think he remembered me, but that didn't matter. I ran out in my bare feet, past my neighbour's house to meet him and found myself saying, 'It must be either leukaemia or an infection.' I said this because I had spent several months as a staff nurse on a leukaemia ward. The doctor just nodded his head and looked very sad.

We sat in our lounge, Russ in the same seat opposite the window where he had sat when the financial advisor had talked to us about personal sickness insurance. He had said to us, 'Like all insurances, where do you stop?' So we had decided to do nothing.

The day of the doctor's visit is as raw and fresh in my mind as though it were yesterday. He wouldn't confirm the diagnosis of leukaemia, but said he was very surprised to see Russ looking so well. He said, 'From your blood result I'd expected you to need immediate admission to hospital, but looking at you now I don't think it'll be necessary.' He asked us to attend an appointment with the haematology consultant in Cheltenham hospital the following morning. And then the doctor was gone. It must have been such a tough visit for him. He had come into a happy home of a 38-year-old father – probably close to his own age – with a wife and two little children. And he had to tell that father he might have a life-threatening illness.

After the doctor left, Russ and I sat looking at each other.

'Well, at least there is something wrong and I wasn't imagining it,' Russ began. 'What a relief they know what it is. Now they can do something.'

'We don't know for sure that it's leukaemia,' I said.

'Let's keep it to ourselves tonight.'

I nodded. 'All right. I'll get us some tea.'

'We'll pray first. We need to put it all into God's hands.'

So we prayed to our Father in heaven, and felt that he understood what we were going through. We got supper, put the two girls to bed and slept in relative peace that night.

When I woke the next morning, the memory of the doctor's visit burst into my mind. In that state of being half awake, half asleep, I desperately wanted it all to be a dream, and at some moments I really believed it was. That was to become a familiar pattern in the year ahead.

After dropping the girls with Russ's brother, we drove to the hospital to meet the consultant. He began by explaining different methods of treatment. He seemed to assume that a diagnosis had been firmly made. When we queried this he just said, 'Oh yes, it is leukaemia.' He told us Russ had chronic myeloid leukaemia and that nobody would be able to tell us how long it had been developing. 'A lot will depend on the stage the disease has reached, and to find that out we'll need to do various tests,' he said.

Then he left us alone for a while in a tiny room with no windows. We sat side by side on two chairs fixed to the wall. That was when I saw tears start to fall down Russ's face. He turned to me. 'I don't want the children not to have a daddy.'

I cried with him and we clung to each other. As a nurse I found myself feeling for him and entering into his world. But by then I don't think I'd really taken much in myself.

I tried to sound positive, 'We'll know more when they've done the tests. There's so much they can do nowadays.' But my words just didn't seem to help.

Before we left the hospital he was put on medication to restore his white cell count.

On our way home we called at our church. A summer fete was in full swing and a group of our friends gathered around us in the vestry and prayed. Philip, a trainee minister, prayed that we would have the sure sense of being under God's protection. He also prayed that God's everlasting arms would undergird us, words from the Old Testament book of Deuteronomy, a prayer which was repeated later by others.

Confronted with our situation, some people said, 'That could be happening to me.' One woman remarked to me how lucky she felt that nothing like this had ever happened to her family. Even at that time, I had reservations about this reaction, knowing that suffering is not always ultimately bad. Even in those darkest, bleakest days after diagnosis I took courage from the fact that Jesus endured unimaginable suffering for me so that, through trusting him, I might have everlasting life.

8

CHANGE

Family, friends and people at our church obviously needed to hear of our situation. We knew this, but we decided from the start that we would say nothing to the girls. At age 4 and 3 we felt they were too young to be burdened with the news that their daddy was seriously ill. And anyway, we thought he was going to get better. The first people we told were Russ's mother and stepfather in St Albans. Even though we played down the facts as much as we could, they were devastated. Because my parents lived a fair distance away, we made the mistake of Russ telling my mum over the phone. Russ knew how well my mum usually coped in a crisis, but this news had a shattering effect and I regretted not being with her when she heard it.

Russ was immediately plunged into treatment, with my life becoming a roller coaster ride which would not seem normal for a very long time. I didn't really question why all this was happening, or why Russ had leukaemia. We had spoken with the consultant and he told us there was no clear reason for Russ's diagnosis. I did wonder if something on the farm or from his life before the farm had triggered it, but I was too busy dealing with the here and now to dwell on the causes. And I didn't blame God, because I was aware that illness was not part of his intention in creating the world. During my two years studying theology, I had wrestled with the question of evil in the world, and had come to understand that God is supremely a God of love; this world isn't perfect, and I didn't assume that my life should be painless when so many others' lives are not.

I knew too that Russ and I didn't need tragic circumstances to make us appreciate our situation. Even though I had sometimes allowed minor decisions and losses to cloud the bigger picture of our life together, I loved being a wife and mum. Sometimes I had felt the need for a bigger challenge, but Russ appreciated every aspect of his present circumstances and was very fulfilled.

Although at that stage we didn't consider that Russ would die, our lives changed irrevocably. Inevitably, we were changing too. But we held on to the fact that God had not changed, and his love and care underpinned our lives. He was the same loving, heavenly Father whom we had grown to know and who was right there with us in our deep valley in a way no human person could be. He knit us together even more closely than before and strengthened us as we looked up to him and not just across to each other for support.

Hospital appointments became a regular part of our routine, and Russ and I made the first of two trips to Southmead Hospital for his white blood cells to be filtered off and new healthy ones infused. Russ was very touched to realize that for him to receive the healthy blood cells, people had gone to the trouble of donating theirs – a more involved procedure than regular blood donation. I was so focused on the practicalities of daily life that I didn't think about the altruism of the donors then. It was more than a year later that it sank in, and I made the decision to donate my own cells in future in recognition of their kindness.

Blood tests and chemotherapy continued for several weeks and we learnt that although the illness itself was at an advanced stage, his condition was still in an early enough phase for various treatments to be considered. To say we were relieved is an understatement. Because he'd been so excessively tired, Russ had reduced his work hours slightly, but he was only too keen to increase them again now that his anaemia and overall blood picture had picked up a bit.

I spoke to a friend one day, and was struck by a particular Bible verse, 'This illness is not unto death' (John 11:4, RSV). I looked in my Bible and discovered that Jesus had said this about Lazarus who suffered 'that the Son of God may be glorified'. I wondered what this could mean for us.

While tidying the bedroom, my eyes fell on a note which I had scribbled before Russ was ill. It referred to disaster passing as the seasons do; despair and crying would give way to praise and trust. As I awoke one morning, my mind echoed the words, 'weeping may remain for a night, but rejoicing comes in the morning' from Psalm 30:5, and I was comforted.

One character in the Bible struck a particular chord with me as I read. The Old Testament character Job seemed to have a really raw deal. He served God, and yet his family and possessions were taken from him. Faithful Job managed to maintain his love of God despite many whys remaining unanswered. Of course, I too could find some whys in my life, but I found Jesus spoke of us having trouble in this world (John 16:33). Eventually, after a very testing time, Job actually received so much more than he had before. I guess I occasionally wondered if that would happen for us.

Right from the start, Russ and I had understood the implications of deciding to follow Christ. We sincerely wanted his glory to be revealed on earth and now wondered if, in some unfathomable way, our testimony to God's faithfulness in adversity might be part of doing that. We knew that Christianity was not an easy road, but were aware that in the book of Acts, Jesus' followers experienced his joy and power in the midst of their hardships.

Russ said to me, 'God doesn't always remove our suffering – although in many parts of the world today, people are being healed and even brought back to life through the power of Christ. Judy, I believe nothing is impossible for God, who has created the world and all of us.' So we persisted in our fervent prayers for healing.

Family and friends became a larger part of our lives, but it did become really tiring to repeat the same news and then hear the phone ring yet again, while still trying to focus on our two lively youngsters. However, because we believed so much in the power of prayer, the knowledge that so many were praying for us meant a tremendous amount. I believe God helped us to take one day at a time and not to panic. In hindsight, I could have asked a few key people to keep others notified of our progress. This worked well with our church, where Ann, the vicar's wife, did an excellent job of letting individuals know. The people who cared for us needed up-to-date news. Although I did my very best, I didn't really have the time or energy to keep our many other friends informed.

Some friends were amazed that we said nothing to the girls. Although Russ and I were dealing daily with medical developments, family life went on as before and

27.6.23 As John Kowowski has been saying about my very many prayers for him, even though he knows only that I'm his niece's next door neighbour.

there was still joy and laughter around the home. We didn't walk around in despair, and we honestly sensed God closer to us than we had ever done; we felt enveloped in his comfort. In a very real sense we felt that Jesus drew near and walked with us, helping us to feel safe and secure even though our circumstances looked scary and unsettled.

Gradually we introduced the girls to the idea of Daddy having to go to the hospital to have blood taken, and they took it in their stride. The consultant needed to monitor the effects of his medication on Russ, and twice a week I drove the family to the hospital before dropping Russ at work.

'Please let us watch, Mummy, please!' begged Rachel and, as they were very interested, the nurses had no choice but to let us all in. The girls calmly watched the blood being taken from their father's arm. So, gradually, they became aware that daddy had 'poorly blood', and the doctors were trying to make it better.

Before long we had to address the urgent issue of looking for a donor match from within Russ's family. We had no idea whether Eira or Phil would prove to be a suitable match to donate their bone marrow to save their brother. Like Russ, Phil had an aversion to needles and hospitals, but he and Eira immediately said they would help if they could.

On the day of the tests, Phil's wife Anne was also with us and I remember how we laughed as we waited, the sun streaming through the large hospital window as Russ and Phil reminisced about boyhood panics over injections. Even in that situation they could find humour.

Russ was given a bone marrow biopsy, and I felt horrified as I heard him cry out when the needle shot though his spine to pinpoint its target, impacting the surrounding tissues. It was really horrible, but at least this ordeal was quickly over – and Russ took the opportunity to tell the consultant about his training as a lay reader.

On the day the test results were due, my parents surprised us with a visit. Dad had planted a splendid display of begonias and busy lizzies around the front of our house and was thrilled to see Russ's appreciation when he returned home from work. We were all in the back garden when the consultant phoned.

'I've got great news for you, Russell. Your brother Phil is a perfect match.'

It was the best thing we could have heard. Russ sat down on the old toy box, choked and overwhelmed. I sobbed, releasing all the pent-up emotion as the amazing news began to sink in.

A few days later, Russ and I drove to Bristol together for an appointment with a consultant at the children's hospital, which was the best place for adults to be treated too. Traffic was terrible and it took an hour and a half to weave through the city and up the very steep St Michael's Hill. We paid an extortionate parking fee, and found ourselves facing a very old Victorian building set back from the road. This was our first sight of the place which held so much promise for us.

The consultant was a tall, friendly man we took an instant liking to; he was someone we felt we could trust. He made it clear that he appreciated how we'd been unaware that anything was seriously wrong with Russ. He said, 'You know, with a young family and a demanding job as well as your lay reader commitments, it's quite understandable you'd feel a healthy tiredness from time to time.'

The consultant wholeheartedly recommended a transplant, although he didn't minimize the risks.

'This could affect every organ of your body,' he told Russ. Then he added, 'Even your brain.'

Those words rang in my head as I struggled to take in the new possibility that our children might have a father with brain damage. One part of me was terrified, but at the same time another part of me was rushing to convince myself we'd deal with it if it happened. I knew that if brain damage did happen, Russ wouldn't be the same as before.

Beside me, Russ nodded. He looked as if he was frantically tried to assimilate this devastating news. After a pause, he went on to ask some questions. We discussed all the possibilities, and were both certain that we wanted to go ahead with the transplant operation. Then we thanked the consultant and got up to leave.

As Russ drove us home, we sat in silence for part of the way. This was one of the few times I remember being overwhelmed by the enormity of our situation. None of it seemed real, and yet it was. I felt sick and unutterably sad; it seemed that the earth had opened up and we were already half way down the blackest hole imaginable. Tears trickled down our faces. It was the second time since his diagnosis that Russ had cried, and I can't even recall the rest of the journey. As we turned the corner into our village, he unexpectedly announced, 'I need to go to the garden centre and buy some stones. I want to lay the patio.'

How could I say, 'No, that's too energetic,' or, 'We can't afford it yet'? So I kept quiet.

Russ continued to go to work, as it was important to him to maintain his sense of identity and continuity. When he shared the news of his illness with his manager and colleagues, they were tremendously supportive. Although new to the job, Russ was well respected. Many people at work were close to him in age, and his news obviously affected them. His direct manager showed incredible strength and understanding, as he was coping with his own cancer remission at that time. *God-given instance at work*

A date was booked for Russ to be admitted to Bristol Royal Hospital for Children for a bone marrow transplant – 15 August. Before that, on a beautiful summer day, our friend, Rob, arrived to help lay our patio. My parents visited in the evening, and we marvelled at the speed and precision with which Russ and Rob were working. We later found that Russ had insisted on doing the majority of the heavy work himself.

The family celebrated with a relaxing meal on the patio, planning to eat the plump fillet steaks brought by my dad with broad beans fresh from his garden. The wine flowed and the lingering scent of flowers wafted on the evening breeze. Although my father is a real expert at cooking steak, he had never used our oven grill; consequently, our peace outside was shattered by a yell of 'Fire!' from the kitchen. Russ remained characteristically calm in his chair, and we all laughed till we hurt – humour is surely a Godsend in times like this.

The first week of August arrived. Russ and I had an evening out together, beginning with a gentle walk on Cleeve Hill, hand in hand. Even though the transplant loomed so large, Russ couldn't resist leaving the path to climb the grassy slopes, and I didn't try to stop him. We then drove into Cheltenham for a Chinese meal, where our tearful eyes met across the table.

After the meal, we strolled through the town. For most of our married life we'd had buggies to push, so we dearly appreciated the chance to walk together. Suddenly, we heard footsteps speeding up behind us. I thought we were in danger, but it was the waitress who was after us, my lipstick in her hand! And so we ended what was to be our last evening out together, laughing.

Russ knew I would be making many journeys to the hospital in Bristol and our car was very old. As we'd been saving towards a replacement for three years, he decided it was time to buy one. We agreed on an economical car which would be easy for me to manoeuvre. He insisted that I drive our new car home from the garage, although it would have been a joy for him. He said, 'This car is really for you and the girls.' On the surface I think he meant that he would take the bus to work, but deep down, although perhaps unacknowledged even to himself, he may have known it was ultimately a car solely for the girls and me.

There were tears in my eyes as I thought about the magnitude of our situation. Few parents at school knew that Rachel's father had leukaemia. A few days before Russ was booked into Bristol, I planned a butterfly and bee dressing-up party for Rachel with twenty children, and accepted help from friends – something I was learning to do. Russ popped in to see everyone on his return from work.

Our two girls delighted in making and drawing, and from time to time I would catch Lucy dipping her fingers in the dregs of her yoghurt and decorating the kitchen table with it. One meal time, Rachel pointed at Lucy's smears and exclaimed, 'Look Mummy, Lucy's making her rainbow!'

Around the same time, Rachel was playing in the garden and suddenly came running to say, 'Mummy, Mummy, a rainbow!' She had created a rainbow in the garden with the hose. The entire rainbow was contained within our garden, and I found myself speaking out those words that had recently sprung out at me, 'This illness is not unto death,' praying earnestly as I spoke.

That summer we kept seeing rainbows, and I feel quite sure that God drew our attention to them. We have a photo of the one in the garden, interpreting it as a special sign of hope for our family, and showing that God had not forgotten us.

I watched Russ playing ball with the girls on the back lawn, grabbed the camcorder and filmed them, assuming that Rachel and Lucy wouldn't see him for several weeks during his treatment. My plan was to show them the film as a reminder of their daddy while he was in hospital.

Little did I realize how precious those minutes of film would be.

9

NOT MUCH OF A HOLIDAY

As Russ drove us to Bristol for a day appointment in early August, we had a debate over what was next on the agenda. His bone marrow transplant was planned for Tuesday 15 August and he would need to be there a week early to begin preparation treatment. We had been told that he would need to be in isolation for up to three weeks afterwards, and the consultant recommended I make daily visits to aid his recovery. The girls would not be allowed into isolation, and I had to arrange care for them. I knew that if they were happy everything would be much easier for me to handle, and I was anxious that our standards of care and discipline would be maintained. So a visit to the hospital playgroup was high on my agenda. Russ didn't see the need for this, and he was understandably preoccupied with his own circumstances.

During our car journey, it hit me that we were approaching his illness from different angles. Although Russ and I were very much united as a couple, my role now lay in supporting him and the girls, whereas his was in coping with his treatment. My new role was just beginning and it felt like stepping into the icy cold of Narnia. I longed for the warmth of the fur coats to envelop me, and I desperately wanted the two of us to be together as we were before. It felt as if I was operating on two levels. One lay in the moment, with the many practicalities and my family to care for; the other in the past. Somehow they were inter-twined, like a strand of bindweed wrapping itself around a rose. I looked for the rose, but all the time it was further away, and inside I went on sobbing for what I'd known and was no more.

Once we arrived, I left Russ in the clinic and went in search of the playgroup. Eventually I found it, and caught sight of the leader wearing a huge fancy dress hat. My first thought was, 'This looks like a place for children to relax and have fun.' The walls were covered with interesting murals, and I could see the cupboards were full of play equipment. From the warm welcome I knew immediately that the girls would be well looked after here. I felt reassured and better able to face what I knew was coming.

After that, it was countdown to transplant.

The unavoidable day arrived for our family to relocate to Bristol. We were delighted to hear we would be offered family accommodation, which meant the girls and I could stay in Bristol instead of driving an hour there and back each day. In the meantime, we were booked into a hotel for the first night. For the hour before leaving home, Russ and I sat together in our tiny study, devising and printing out a prayer diary for the people who wanted to pray for us. It was important to us to give them clear guidelines – for example, to pray about the specific reactions which were most likely to occur immediately after the transplant. The diary included key dates in Russ's treatment, and some of the

Bible verses which people had shared with us as they had prayed about Russ. We were so very grateful to family and friends here and abroad for their prayers, love and practical care for us.

When we arrived in Bristol, we drove straight to our hotel, and in the evening we strolled to the quayside. As we ate a takeaway, Russ smiled at the girls and joked, 'Hey, you two, this isn't much of a holiday!'

They laughed, not really understanding the joke, as it felt like a holiday to them.

When we got back to our hotel, an austere building looming large on the corner of a spacious road, I had the worst night of our whole time in Bristol. It was very, very hot. I unpacked the girls' nightclothes and put them on their beds next to ours.

I said to Russ, 'I have to find some milk for the girls. I'm going down to reception to see if I can buy some. I'll be as quick as I can.'

The girl on reception suggested I find a kitchen and look there. I went back upstairs and pushed my way through numerous fire doors to the kitchen, where I took the lids off thirty little sachets of milk to make a drink for the girls. On my way back to the room I got lost, and found myself staring at a door leading onto the roof. Desperately searching for our corridor, my situation seemed to mirror my life just then – ahead of me was an unknown path to an unknown destination.

Back in the hotel room, Russ was hot and disgruntled. 'Why have you taken so long? The girls wanted you and I kept saying you'd be back any minute. You've been ages.'

'I couldn't find the milk. It was awful. I got lost and kept banging into fire doors – loads of them. I couldn't find my way.'

'Where's my green shirt? I need it for tomorrow.'

He seemed totally unmoved by my struggle, and this was very unlike him.

I got the shirt and put the girls to bed. It took ages as they were so excited to be in a hotel. It was a game to them.

Suddenly I yelped, 'Oh, my word, we can't have that!'

'What?' Russ looked up from his Bible, which was carefully propped open on the table next to his *Autocar* magazine.

'We can't have that sash window open. There's a big gap at the bottom. What if they fell out?'

'They won't fall out.'

'They might. I can't have it. I know you're hot. But I can't have it.' I closed the window and tried to pull the top part down instead. It hardly moved. I felt exhausted and tears pricked my eyes.

Pulling the sheet over me I called out and asked God to help us.

Next morning, I looked down from the window to wave to Russ. He had an early check-in and felt it would be easier for him to walk the short distance alone rather than dragging us all out. He had his black zipped holdall flung over his shoulder, one of four cases given to us as a wedding present. He smiled and waved, disappearing into the distance.

Our friends Jackie and Jerry had offered to put us up for the weekend as our hospital accommodation still wasn't ready. Russ was to be allowed out for most of the time at this point, so we all spent a few days at their delightful rambling cottage in Nailsworth, and Jackie drove Russ to the hospital early one morning. Their support was such a help, particularly as I now had a bout of food poisoning and felt very rough. Jackie and Jerry had two little girls who played well, albeit noisily, with ours. I felt that God knew our needs and he met them through our friends, who were unfazed by our situation.

Our final move was into a little bedsit in a large Victorian terraced house for relatives, near to the hospital, transferring to a top floor flat after a couple of weeks. The girls adapted to their new surroundings readily. We enjoyed afternoon walks together in the nearby university grounds between Russ's hospital appointments.

By now he had to follow a special diet – a challenge in itself – and planning ahead was hard, for we never knew what the next day would bring. When I eventually had some quiet time in the evening, I was exhausted after all the juggling of the day, and I found phone calls very draining. Nevertheless, I valued the love and concern of friends and family, appreciating that they needed to know what was happening and wanted to know what to pray for.

One weekend, Liz, my school friend of over thirty years, travelled over to take care of the girls and give me a break. Knowing they were safe, I relished the chance to spend more time beside Russ's bed. Together we updated our prayer sheet and sent copies to friends around the world. That same evening, a friend suggested we read Psalm 91, and we were comforted to read of being in the 'shelter of the Most High' (v.1). Russ felt he certainly was being protected. He turned to me and said, 'I love you.'

He had not always found those words easy to say, although he had certainly shown his love in so many ways, and shared it in handwritten valentine love poems.

'Darling, I so appreciate you being with me through all of this. Thank you for all you're doing.'

I pushed the table away from the bed to get closer and said, 'I love you very, very much, more than ever,' and I looked deep into his eyes for what seemed an age.

That night I read myself to sleep with excerpts from *A Very Present Help*, by the missionary Amy Carmichael.

Amy spent the last twenty years of her life bedridden in India, and I felt encouraged and reassured by her certainty that God's love and faithfulness remains firm through our times of trial.

All too soon came the day for Russ to go into isolation. The consultant encouraged me to stay for as long as possible when I went to see him.

'I think the emotional benefit of your visits, Mrs Hopkins, far outweighs any chance of infection. The main risk is from Russ's own body.'

Although the girls were not allowed into his room we found an interesting ramble through bushes to his window, which meant they could see him and speak on a mobile phone. Russ's mum had the great idea of carrying her own chair to this window when she visited.

During the next few weeks as family visited, Russ had a constant stream of window visitors. I was thrilled to have my family over from the States. It meant such a lot to Russ to see my brother and sister-in-law and their two children. We were allowed to choose three additional named people who would be allowed into the isolation chamber, and we chose our vicar and Phil and his wife, Anne, who were able to make regular visits from Cheltenham during the transplant.

Phil had now donated his bone marrow ready for the transplant, and after following a strict diet before the operation, he said he was determined to convince the nursing staff, that like him, Russ should drink a carton of vegetable juice and a pint of stout a day. The consultant later told him his was one of the best samples of marrow they'd ever had!

Meanwhile, family life went on. I found a small supermarket up the road, which I visited most days. Gazing at the fruit and vegetables, my mind whirling, I thought, 'My husband's very ill and we don't know what's going to happen.' Every few days I trudged down tiny streets with the girls to the launderette and took my place next to students and other mothers. It was strange to think I had my own washing machine at home, but didn't know when I would use it again.

I chose a good church around the corner, and managed a Sunday morning or two in the congregation while the girls were at the kids' club. People I spoke to over coffee were shocked to hear about our situation and several offered meals; I never took them up on it. I didn't know how the week would go, and lived day to day.

Despite our situation, I made sure the children had fun. I took them to parks, and when my parents visited, the girls relished travelling on an open-top bus all together and eating sugar lumps sneaked to them under the table by my father. Rachel enjoyed the little school at the hospital, although she much preferred the times she was allowed into Lucy's playgroup. On the occasions when the playgroup had room for both our children, I would often surprise Russ with an afternoon bedside visit. I loved that and he did too.

So those first weeks passed as an adventure for the girls, but not much of a holiday for Russ and me.

10

TRANSPLANT

A bone marrow transplant involves the donor marrow being given to the patient by venous infusion over several hours, and the actual event seems surprisingly simple. Russ's transplant was characteristically uneventful and it left him with no immediate ill-effects.

A few days later he had a bad day – he didn't seem himself, and asked me to deal with some financial matters, which we had always done together. This episode of backing off from responsibility went on for two days and it is hard for me to describe the feelings I experienced, having Russ present, but not being fully with me. I suppose it was a kind of loss, a bereavement in itself, as I suddenly realized that part of the way we dealt with life together had already altered. He had changed, and I had no way of knowing if this was the tip of an iceberg, submerged but about to loom up large as we came closer to our destination.

At this point, I spotted a woman in the street who reminded me of someone I knew back home who was bringing up her child alone. I had sometimes felt wistful for the closeness she had with her daughter, and it now struck me that I could cope in a similar situation. The thought surprised me, and I wondered whether God was beginning to prepare me for what lay ahead.

Rachel and Lucy were adapting well to their father's situation. After the birth of the girls, we had adopted the traditional pattern of husband as breadwinner and wife as homemaker. After working for sixteen years, I loved having a home and family of my own, and was more than ready to shoulder most of the childcare. Russ, on the other hand, was growing into his profession and had increasing preaching responsibilities. It had been a joy for me to see him progress, and as he needed to rest on coming home, the children were used to my making supper and putting them to bed.

Rachel and Lucy obviously missed their father coming in and having fun with them, but they had actually seen more of him in the last few months and now knew exactly where he was all the time. I found it a bonus having Russ nearby all day, although I didn't appreciate the circumstances. But the girls were on an adventure, and were revelling in the attention lavished on them by the staff. They received so much help, from Lorraine on reception smiling every morning and saying, 'Good morning, princesses!' as we climbed the hospital steps, to the excellent input by skilled play therapists who explained what was happening physically to their father, using dolls and bandages.

I could cope with brief and caring phone conversations, although there never did seem to be a good time to receive them. I just wanted rest, space, and the assurance of people's prayers. Letters helped us both enormously, especially those bringing spiritual hope and comfort. It was also nice to receive a gift in the post such as Rombouts coffee or a special packet of biscuits. Treats such as a meal out with my parents or a boat trip with the girls seemed like wonderful oases in the desert at this time. I occasionally took time out just for me when the girls were both at playgroup. I had a swim in a nearby pool, or a chocolate bomb dessert at a nearby café; once I treated myself to a blue cardigan from Monsoon. Phil and Anne made sure that Russ had a box of chocolates ready for me on my birthday, which almost made up for the fact that he had forgotten. He had never missed one before.

On three evenings a week, Radio Lollipop Club was run in the hospital by a team of volunteers. They took over three rooms at the end of a long corridor, filled with fun activities. Rachel learnt to make animal creations from balloons, and Lucy acquired her dominant memory of Bristol – playing in the ball pit with a new little friend. I was full of gratitude for all that the girls received from Radio Lollipop and, while they were happily immersed for an hour or two on an evening, I grabbed the opportunity to sit with Russ.

On one of those occasions, after sterilizing my hands and putting on a sterile dress and clean shoes outside his isolation room as usual, he greeted me with a twinkling smile.

In a very matter-of-fact way he began to describe his remarkable experience of that afternoon: 'I was lying on my bed, resting. I wasn't asleep, just closing my eyes, when I suddenly felt there were lots of people around my bed. I knew that was strange as only one or two members of staff ever come in here together. So I opened my eyes but there was nobody there. As soon as I closed my eyes, the feeling came back. Three times I opened my eyes and, as before, no one was there. Then I realized, that all around me were angels! Every now and then, I actually sensed one of them was bending over to tend to me.'

Ten minutes later, Russ and I were enjoying a TV programme together in his room – and nothing could have felt less ethereal and other-worldly. Although I didn't doubt his account of the experience, on my way out, I checked with the staff whether Russ had been given any hallucinogenic drugs. He hadn't.

Russ's experience of the angels stayed fresh in our minds, but it was only very recently that I realized that Psalm 91, which my friend had sent, speaks in verse 11 of God commanding his angels 'to guard you in all your ways'. That small hospital room will always remain in my memory as a place where heaven came down to touch earth, we were so very conscious of the presence of God there. In a strange sense, both Russ and I loved to be there.

Russ surprised the doctors and staff by requiring only mild analgesia after the transplant, and I put it down to his determination to avoid drugs more than to a lack of pain. Equally, he resisted special liquid feeding up to the very day when weight loss would finally make it necessary. When that day arrived, unbeknown to me, during my visit he cheekily beckoned to me to pass him the auroscope (which consists of a magnifying lens and light; it is used for examining the external ear), which he then quickly tucked into his pocket. He nodded his head to indicate that he wanted the other small items from the table, which again went straight into his pocket. Puzzled, I went along with this bizarre behaviour until the nurse walked in clutching the scales.

Russ climbed on, and she immediately expressed surprise at his weight gain! He did confess what he'd done, but still managed to escape the liquid feeding as his weight had, fortunately, begun to improve.

One day he teased me by saying he was plotting to remove the cupboard shelves in his isolation room so he could hide in there when the nurse was due. I was thrilled to see the old twinkle in his eye. I couldn't imagine life without him; we fitted together like a hand in a glove.

When a volunteer offered him a massage, asking how he would rate his stress levels on a scale of one to ten (with ten being the most relaxed), Russ decided on nine! I don't think she was used to having that kind of reply. He suggested I have the massage instead, and I could certainly have done with it!

The doctors had indicated that Russ was ready to come out of isolation, and we were eagerly waiting for confirmation during the doctor's round. Our friend Fiona, back in England on leave from her children's orphanage in Zimbabwe, had driven down to be with us for a few days, and we were in the park with the children when Russ phoned from hospital to say he was ready. I drove straight there and found him sitting waiting for me. We hadn't expected his discharge so early in the day, and I felt sad that I had kept him waiting on his first day of freedom.

Together we walked up the hill to our temporary home, and Russ had his first opportunity to appreciate the early autumnal air. The isolation had been cut short by three days as he was progressing so well. But when the consultant had spoken of Russ's condition I felt there was a bit of a proviso. 'Your husband is doing very well today.' I didn't like the use of the word 'today'.

As we approached the entrance to our flat, the words of John Bunyan's hymn echoed in my mind, 'To Be a Pilgrim'. I hadn't thought of that hymn since I was at school, and believed God had brought it to my mind, as I considered how Russ was intent on following Christ despite his circumstances.

Russ wanted to surprise the girls, so I hadn't told them of his homecoming. He rang the bell and Rachel, as the oldest, asked Fiona's permission to open the door. She was excited but a little overwhelmed to see her daddy, and her small hand found her favourite spot, enveloped in his. Later on, she used her teddy bear to communicate her feelings: 'Toby Bear didn't want you to go into hospital. Toby Bear is happy for you to be out.' Lucy was equally delighted to see her father, and quickly found her place on his lap.

The next few weeks revolved around the flat, daily clinic visits, school, playgroup and walks to the nearby college grounds. We took seriously the medical advice to avoid crowded places. Russ had to follow a strict diet, and I searched the little supermarket for appropriate meals. I needed to buy certain packets of ready-made meals to heat up. We ate many things we'd never had before, always thinking them too expensive and less healthy than home-cooked meals. I gazed at the supermarket shelves knowing this was a new kind of food shopping for me, and wondering when he would eat 'normally' again.

At daily clinic check-ups, Russ chatted away to other post-transplant patients and I was always struck by his determination as he spoke of building up his exercise regime. Looking back, I sometimes wonder if he overdid things, but my fretful questions have decreased in intensity as time has passed.

One quiet morning we visited the nearby museum on Queen's Road, where Russ delighted in showing the girls part of a dinosaur bone. Amongst all of this, I kept up with the daily chores such as washing, cleaning and letting people know how Russ was doing.

This period of time was much more critical than the transplant, for it was now that the life-threatening complication of graft-versus-host disease could set in. A mild form could be seen as favourable proof that the transplant was becoming established. But a more serious reaction would indicate rejection of the new bone marrow.

It was during this time that we heard the shocking news from America that my brother, Nick, had suffered a heart attack. He was just 43, pretty fit, and in the middle of an organized ten-mile run when it happened. His heart had a 90 per cent blockage on the right side, and this could have cost him his life. In the space of a few months, both my husband and only sibling might have died. Fortunately, Nick was treated promptly and began a full recovery.

After these first few weeks, it gradually became apparent that Russ was, in fact, developing a graft-versus-host reaction. His skin was mildly affected first, but then he began to feel really ill as his intestine became involved. The medical staff felt that Russ should remain in our flat, as there he would be least vulnerable to infection, yet close enough to walk to the clinic daily.

Those days and nights were the most difficult and uncertain we had faced. But during this time, we felt God with us, and knew he would never desert us. We would encourage each other with words from the Bible, saying that if we draw near to him, then he will draw near to us (see Jas. 4:8, NKJV). Sometimes we felt him reassure us, as a Bible passage or verse stood out from the others. At other times it seemed that God had prompted an individual to pray, write or speak words of encouragement to us. In our hearts and tangibly, we felt his Holy Spirit acting.

In the apartment, Russ preferred to sleep in the lounge on a put-up bed, as he could then easily reach the bathroom without disturbing me. This arrangement gave him more space and suited him, although I found it hard, as I wanted to be next to him.

It was a sad night when the doctor phoned us and said, 'I'm going to have to put Russ on steroids. I know how much you wanted to avoid this, but I really feel this is the best course of action now.'

The staff remained optimistic and didn't anticipate side-effects from the steroids, such as swelling. By now Russ's hair was falling out but he insisted on hanging on to the last few strands. About five weeks after the transplant, the steroids began to have a marked effect, and Russ began to feel so much better that we were allowed to return home to Cheltenham for a night.

We told very few people of our brief return home, and we were anxious to avoid a great celebration as we knew we weren't out of danger yet. Right from the start we had emphasized that the crucial time would be the weeks after the transplant rather than the event itself; yet people understandably believed that the worst was over, and some who saw us were jubilant.

Russ was perched on the kitchen stool, glancing through one of several free newspapers our neighbour had stacked on the bin. I accidentally knocked some tins over, and grumbled, 'I've said again and again that the transplant is not the real danger. Why don't people get it?'

'It's human nature to hone in on the action instead of what happens after.'

'It annoys me!'

He looked up briefly. 'Judy,' he said. 'Don't be too hard on people.'

On the Saturday morning Russ even sneaked a drive out in the new car. 'I'm just popping out for petrol, darling.' He did get petrol but also happened to call in to the car park of his old work colleagues a few miles away to give them an update.

'Does Judy know about this?' Joe asked.

'Oh, it's fine,' said Russ, very quickly. He went on to show his colleague he was still streaks ahead in the hair front, as he still had a few strands compared to Joe.

I was actually pleased to get back to the cocoon of the Bristol flat that Sunday evening. At home I had ventured to the shops, hoping to remain anonymous as I felt too emotionally vulnerable to answer questions. Home-making now seemed easier for me in Bristol, although Russ's delight at being back in Cheltenham had made the trip worthwhile. He'd often urged me to pop back for a day, but I hadn't wanted to go without him, even for a few hours.

Not long after our weekend trip home, I noticed that Russ's face was getting rounder. He seemed unperturbed by this, perhaps he was unaware of it, and the girls just saw him as their same daddy.

One tea time, Russ decided to get rid of his last locks of hair and called the girls to sit next to each other on the burgundy carpet in our main room. They opened their eyes wide as he shaved off the remaining strands. Dancing, clapping, and shrieking, 'Hurrah!', Rachel suddenly stopped and said, 'Daddy's going to have to wear his cap now when it gets cold.'

11

A BREAK IN THE CLOUDS

September was drawing to a close, and the leaves on the trees were beginning to change colour with the start of autumn. Every day Russ ambled down the road from our flat to the hospital for his check-ups.

Family and friends were in touch, and my sister-in-law, Jackie, even offered to fly over from the States to be with us. Russ considered this, but knew we would be stretched for space in the flat. He was secure with his established routine and I understood his need for this, with so much uncertainty around him. I would have loved to have her help and support, but his happiness was paramount. Somehow, too, I sensed a deep preciousness in our time together; we had come this far as a family unit, and I wanted to hold on to that, having no idea what tomorrow would bring.

We were very tired and to a certain extent we had cut ourselves off from other people in order to be able to function. On the few occasions when the girls were in playgroup in the afternoon, we stole a precious hour and a half together. Russ was determined to maintain exercise by regularly walking to the end of Queen's Road –

quite a distance from the hospital – and then adamantly refusing to take a taxi back. He just wasn't used to taking them. Sometimes he would be exhausted when we returned.

The graft-versus-host condition was not easing as quickly as hoped, and the steroids were increased, although the doctors still thought it would be best for Russ to remain with us in the flat. He insisted on taking charge of his medicines and regular temperature checks, which annoyed me at times, as I felt sure I could have done this in a more relaxed way. More recently I've realized that so much control was being taken away from Russ that he needed to hang on to this last area.

A couple of incidents stick in my mind from this time. Two students once walked past Russ and me on a narrow street. They glanced at Russ, fell silent, and gave us a wide berth. I looked at my husband and realized that just three months earlier those students would probably have expected us to move. But now, due to the steroids, he bore more than a passing resemblance to the Incredible Hulk, enhanced by his refusal to wear a cap and a recent habit of pulling his coat sleeves down to the very tips of his fingers.

At the time I suppressed my own painful feelings about Russ's changing appearance, and it was only much later that I was able to confide in a friend how difficult it had been to take in. I loved him just the same, if not more, but it was heart-wrenching to look at him and see that he no longer looked like my Russ.

The second memorable incident happened on his daily walk to his appointment at the clinic. His insistence on going alone concerned me, but it wasn't ideal for me to accompany him, as I had a toddler and buggy to negotiate, and we could have knocked him off balance. But as I had become increasingly alarmed by his deteriorating condition, I phoned the staff on one occasion to ask them to look out for him, feeling dreadful going behind his back. The nurse understood my concern and phoned me on his arrival. Later, he admitted to having almost fallen on the zebra crossing on his return journey. 'Judy, it's strange and horrible to be 38 years old and crossing the road like a frail old man, and it's all happened in just a couple of months.'

Russ had been told that he could go home for a day on Saturday 7 October and he was really looking forward to it. As he fell asleep on the Friday night, we were both aware of the increased swelling in his legs, but assumed all was well. The next morning he woke me.

'Judy, I can't move my legs.'

I rang the hospital, and staff promptly sent two porters to bring him down the stairs. By the time they arrived, Russ was actually crying. He was realizing that the medication was having significant side-effects.

'Judy,' he cried, 'I'm afraid I'm going to end up as a lump of meat on a table.'

In the meantime, Rachel had wet the bed.

When Russ had gone, I sorted the girls out and took them, plus the sheets balanced on the buggy, to the launderette, making the return journey one hour later. I telephoned the staff. One of them had been reassuring Russ, for which I was grateful. He had been frightened and the nurse, suddenly remembering his faith, had said, 'You're a Christian, aren't you? We'll call the hospital chaplain.'

It was a great relief for Russ to speak with this man, and in no time at all, he was enthusiastically sharing the story of his conversion with him.

The chaplain said, 'You're a computer man, so you should write all this down.'

And that's how this book was conceived.

The staff were now so concerned about Russ's condition that he was transferred to Frenchay Hospital. I was enormously grateful to the mother of Lucy's new little friend, who offered to take the girls so I could drive there to see him. When I arrived it felt as if I had gone back in time – as if I were in one of those TV programmes where people step back a few generations. The surroundings seemed old-fashioned. Russ was in one of many single-storey wards, and the feel of the place was homely and unthreatening. Anxious as I was, this helped me as I weaved my way through the warren-like pathways to locate Russ's ward.

The nurse in charge told me they had reduced his steroids, and I wondered what condition I would find him in. I thought, 'What will he look like? Will he be able to move?' But when I reached the ward, I was stunned to find a scene of complete tranquillity. Russ lay on his bed, looking like the man I had married seven years before, not the ailing invalid of the previous night. And that's when he told me of his vision of the gates of hell, and how he met with Jesus – just as I mentioned in the introduction.

Later Russ spoke of how this incident had started a softening of his heart, meaning he could draw alongside people in a new and deep way. I could see the evidence of this myself as I watched him relating to other people. He also said that in those moments of such intimacy with Christ, he prayed for our church to grow.

Shortly afterwards Russ was taken back to the children's hospital in Bristol in an emergency ambulance, while I followed in my car. Now he was happy and relaxed, really enjoying the mode of transport. When he got out he said, 'It felt as if I was in a James Bond movie.'

It turned out that Russ needed an emergency local operation as his Hickman line in his chest had become infected. It was through the Hickman line that all his drugs were administered. This is a fairly common complication after transplant. Later that evening, the registrar phoned me to say, 'Mrs Hopkins, it has been a privilege and delight to operate on your husband.' A nurse told me how Russ had been asking the staff about their holidays and how everyone had been touched by his concern for them and his obvious *joie de vivre*.

The following week passed by quite smoothly. Russ had a wonderful room with a high, soft bed which the girls loved to climb on. He phoned my mum to say, 'You should see my five star accommodation. It's amazing!'

I was buoyed up by a visit from Ann, our vicar's wife, and Marc, a fellow member of our church. After giving me valuable help with the children and around the flat, they walked down the hill to see Russ. It was sixteen years since Marc had first knocked on Russ's bedsit door, hours after his conversion experience on the hill, and had invited Russ to hear the evangelist Billy Graham in Bristol. That was where Russ had got up out of his seat and joined thousands in the arena to declare his intention to follow Christ. I thought how special it would be for him to see Russ now, back in Bristol, but radiant and totally at peace. None of us knew that this would be the last time Marc would see Russ on earth. Both he and Ann were amazed at Russ's appearance, and both felt sure that God had met with him in a special way.

When they got back to our apartment, Marc told me how Russ, choked up and near to tears, had shared the vision just as he had done with me. Marc said, 'It seems to me that his experience began in a vivid and frightening way – Russ said he thought he was about to be catapulted into hell. But at the very gates there was Jesus, barring the way.'

'That's when the focus of the vision changed,' Ann piped up, 'and it *was* a vision, Judy. Russ shed tears for what it cost Jesus to die for him, to save him from hell. It was a total privilege to hear him speaking like that.'

Because of Russ's situation we hadn't been able to accept all the kind offers from friends to visit us. But the local Mothers' Union suggested they could sit with the children so I could attend evening church services. However, before I could settle into making contact with people there, suddenly we heard that Russ was to be discharged.

My initial feeling was of total disbelief, as he could hardly walk and had even requested that the discharge date be delayed by a few days. But he seemed overjoyed now and in high spirits. I understood how the condition of transplant patients can alter rapidly from one day to the next and, depending on blood results and other investigations, patients can be sent home and seen as outpatients even though they're not fully well. Very often the home environment is safer, and I would have felt selfish insisting he stay longer in hospital. Anyway, I trusted that we were in the hands both of God and the medical staff.

My parents visited hospital the weekend before Russ's discharge from in- to outpatient. It was the first time Mum had seen Russ with no hair and, since he was back on steroids, his face had started to swell again. When she walked into the hospital room I saw her jaw tighten. As she approached the bed she looked down, skimming her fingers along two plastic bedside tables. She moved slowly, deliberately, pressing more firmly as she got closer. Then she smiled and looked up.

'Hello, love.' She bent over to kiss him. 'It's so good to see you.'

'Hello, Pauline.'

She beckoned to my dad. 'Brian, come and sit down.'

I felt my mouth dry up. Mum looked shocked, ill-equipped to handle the scene she found herself in. As I watched my mum struggling with her emotions, I asked myself why I hadn't foreseen this situation and why I hadn't prepared her better. The girls and I had watched Russ change on a daily basis. Mum hadn't had this luxury.

After the news of Russ's discharge I had only had two days to clear the flat, sort the girls out and tie up all the loose ends. The hospital helped me fill in a form for attendance allowance, which I would be entitled to as Russ's carer in the time before he could return to work. Russ and I had always shied away from claiming any benefits for his condition, but I now realized it was necessary. One line that had been written on the form gave me a powerful jolt; he could have an infection at any time, which could prove fatal.

The discharge date was Monday 23 October 2000 and Russ was so eager to be ready and off early that he asked the staff to find me. He was delighted as the latest positive blood result meant he could immediately leave the ward. I double-checked with the staff, and when I was late in collecting him, he was unusually short with me, saying, 'Judy, I don't see why you had to clean the flat from top to bottom. I just want to get home.'

I could see his point and knew he couldn't begin to understand all that was involved for me as carer for him and our two girls, but his reaction jolted me.

A nurse came with us to the car. I was pushing Lucy in the buggy with little Rachel tottering alongside. When Russ staggered a little, I asked the nurse if she would support his arm.

'Do you want me to, Russ?' she asked him.

'No, I'm fine,' he replied.

I felt undermined and sidelined for that moment.

Nursing at the Sue Ryder.

Mushroom grower.

Love it here.

The helmet at my door.

My valentine.

Happiness 1993.

And then there were two.

So happy together.

Swinging with daddy.

Pooh bear.

Daddy's girls.

Leaving for Bristol.

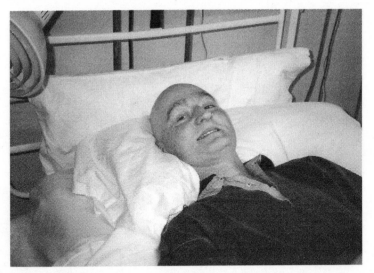

This is going to transform my ministry.

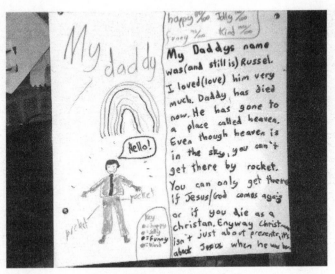

Rachel's drawing board.

Joy of the Lord 2001.

Coping 2002.

Still wearing his jacket.

Pop and Nanan's 2004.

The Hopkins' at home 2011.

Looking forward.

Our car was completely packed with most of the belongings we had collected in the last two and a half months. As I drove down the steep hill, Russ and I said to each other that we sensed the purpose behind our being stopped from leaving Bristol as originally planned. In the early days of the transplant, we had felt that it had somehow gone too well for us. Russ said, 'If that had carried on, we'd probably have been caught up with normal life straight away, and the transplant would have been a mere blip in our lives.'

We both knew that things were now very different and our lives would never be the same again. God had revealed himself to us and touched our lives in a very deep way, and we felt we had a responsibility to use what we had experienced in the future.

As we drove home Rachel cried because she didn't want to leave Radio Lollipop. She was so fond of the volunteers and the treats children were given from little numbered drawers. It seemed as abrupt an exit for her as for me, but I reassured her, 'We'll be back very soon, and Daddy will be back for lots more visits. We haven't left the hospital for good.'

'Yes,' remarked Russ, 'we have to be back at the hospital tomorrow. I have a dental appointment.'

'Russ, I can't believe it!' I said, feeling really angry. 'It's nearly 5 o'clock and it's the rush hour. Why couldn't we stay the night at the flat and leave tomorrow?'

I was exhausted and knew the journey would take us two hours. I went on grumbling, as we stopped at yet another red light. 'In fact, today we were offered a downstairs flat, but you refused and said you were determined to go home.'

'That was because I didn't want to put people out. Today is the day we are going home. And it's important for you that I get you away from here now.'

I felt the stamp of godly authority on his words. But as we drove on to the motorway I went over the mixture of emotions I was feeling – that I was used to Bristol, and reluctant to return to Cheltenham when Russ had only just recovered from a debilitating septicaemic infection. But Russ couldn't hide his excitement. As I moaned and groaned, he said to me, 'This is our homecoming. Please be happy.'

So I decided to be happy, for him.

12

HOMECOMING

As we pulled into our drive I thought the house looked prettier than I'd ever seen it before. The hanging baskets were still full of late colour, and seemed to have made an end of season attempt to welcome us. This was partly due to the kindness of our neighbours, Shirley and Tony, who had watered them and mown our lawn while we'd been away.

Russ turned to me and for the first time ever, congratulated me on my driving. 'You drove beautifully, darling.'

I helped him up the stairs before bringing in the girls and the bags. As I took care of Russ, I could hear Rachel and Lucy unpacking in the messy way that only a 3 and a 5-year-old can. In no time at all, our possessions from the time in Bristol were scattered around the sitting room floor.

No sooner had I mentioned to Russ that we needed milk, than Shirley appeared on the doorstep holding a couple of pints. When I told Russ, he said, 'Good, I was just talking to God about that.' Although he was committed to following Christ before all this, he wasn't usually as

spontaneous and I smiled to see how God had done a special work in his heart that last week in Bristol.

Over a luscious salmon ready-meal in bed he told me
how wonderful it felt to be home, and how much he
appreciated all I was doing. Then a significant thing
happened. Unprompted, each of the girls in turn came in
to spend time alone with their father. Russ must have
realized this was very precious because the next day at
hospital I noticed how his eyes shone as he told the registrar about it.

I've wondered over and over again whether Russ
sensed he might be close to death. He showed no sign of
it and was happily teasing the girls, saying, 'You
thought your daddy was gone – but he's back!' But God
certainly did know, and I can see now how he was guiding us. Shirley later told me, 'Judy, when I saw Russ
coming down the stairs I thought they had sent him
home to die.' But I knew the hospital staff certainly
didn't see it that way.

I can only describe the following day as crazy. When
we woke, Russ told me he could hardly move his legs,
yet he insisted this was quite normal for that time in the
morning. I accepted his explanation and rescheduled his
appointment at the dentist in Bristol from the morning
to the afternoon. I considered ringing around to organize local care for the girls to save them the long car journey but, ridiculous as it may seem, I just couldn't face
asking outright for help. It seemed simpler to take them
with us back to Bristol.

It was Shirley who suggested that Russ would need a
wheelchair. Again, I don't know why it hadn't occurred
to me, but the exhaustion and continuing emotional
stress was stopping me from seeing things clearly. Even
with his obvious physical limitations we had been planning to arrive in Bristol and walk down the hill from our

familiar car park to the dental hospital. Now, seeing the sense of Shirley's advice, we requested a wheelchair when we arrived.

The appointment was uneventful and I was then asked to take him to the outpatient department to see the registrar. We were early. A couple of nurses we had come to know were there.

'Why don't you pop out and do a bit of shopping, Judy?' they asked. 'Russell will be fine with us.'

I took their advice and pushed Lucy up the hill, with young Rachel marching alongside, clasping the handle of the pushchair. I went into the same local supermarket I had used for two months and puzzled over the choice of flowers for the nurses as a thank you for all they had done for us.

'I won't be coming here again so much,' I thought, placing two bunches of pinks and roses on the checkout. 'He'll have less and less appointments and I can get all I need at home. Everything's happening so quickly. Can't really take it in.'

I spent too long choosing a CD birthday present for my nephew, and two pieces of dolls' house furniture for the girls. When we returned, somewhat tired, Russ was in good spirits. Although he'd eaten some food, he looked quite jaded. The nurses loved the flowers and hugged us.

After a little while, the hospital registrar came in, and assessed Russ's temperature and blood pressure. She looked over his blood results and asked, 'Do you feel that your being in a wheelchair may be a step backwards, Mr Hopkins?'

Russ replied, 'No!'

There was no sense in which he was giving in to defeat, and I knew he was as determined as ever to press on to better health and full recovery. And so we returned home to Cheltenham again, in a positive frame of mind and looking forward to another blissful night's sleep in our new bed.

When we woke next day, Wednesday 25 October, Russ said, 'I was really hot in the night.'

I looked at him. 'Why didn't you wake me up?'

'Because I thought it would pass – and it did.' He seemed fine and sat up in bed to devour his three Weetabix with gusto.

I went back downstairs and rummaged around in a kitchen cupboard for a silver whistle and took it up to him. 'Now, please whistle if you need me. That's the only way I will leave you to go downstairs and sort out the girls. Promise?'

'OK, but I feel fine now.'

I wasn't expecting him to use the whistle. I went downstairs and phoned Ann, the vicar's wife, to accept her offer that morning to come and help with the girls so I could give Russ more attention.

Suddenly I heard the shrill note of the whistle. Rushing upstairs, the scene that met my eyes shocked me to the core. Russ looked absolutely dreadful, and whispered to me, 'I'm not very good.' I took his temperature, which was 38 degrees centigrade. Any rise in temperature in a transplant patient can be a serious sign of deterioration. I phoned the registrar in Bristol and told her what was happening. She advised me to wait a short while, just as my guidelines had said, retake his temperature, and ring back. By this time his temperature had virtually gone back to normal, but she nevertheless advised me to dial 999 for an ambulance to Bristol, and to call in at my local hospital en route as a precaution.

Russ and I prayed as I prepared his things. In my hurry and desperation I kept bumping into his feet which were hanging over the end of the bed. It was terrible to hear him yell in pain every time.

When the ambulance arrived, Russ lost consciousness twice while the paramedics helped him on to the stretcher seat and down the stairs. I looked at him and then straight at them, aghast. They tried to reassure me by saying, 'This is not unusual after a transplant, try not to worry.' But I was desperately anxious, asking myself, 'Can this really be happening? Four months ago we were laughing and joking at this same door as if we didn't have a care in the world. Now you are really ill, and being taken out of the house on a stretcher.' Nothing felt real.

After that, everything happened so quickly, like the last grains of sand rushing through an hour glass the minute you look away. Just as Russ was being carried into the back of the ambulance, Ann arrived with a friend to care for the girls. She rushed forward to press the latest copy of *Autocar* in his hands. Russ had come round by then and gave her a broad grin. The paramedics asked if I wanted to take my car. I had no idea. I looked at Russ and climbed into the ambulance, slipping quickly into the seat beside him. I would think about how to get back later. This moment was what mattered and my place was with Russ.

As we drove away in the ambulance, I had no idea that this was the end of life as I knew it. We would never again come home together. Russ was not going to come home at all.

13

TRIUMPH OVER DEATH

When we arrived at Cheltenham hospital the medical staff had a quick look at Russ and realized he was seriously ill. They admitted him as they wanted to start treatment immediately and not spend over an hour getting him to Bristol. They began to make arrangements to move him to intensive care.

While they did this, he was put into one of a series of single rooms around a central desk. The staff made several calls to Bristol to ascertain exactly what had been happening to Russ before his discharge. His Bristol consultant was away, but the registrar was very helpful. Russ was quickly started on medication, but it had to be given slowly and each administration seemed to me to take ages. I stared intently at the fine tube carrying the drugs into his body, as if I could somehow speed it up with the force of my gaze by willing it to go faster. It seemed like a couple of hours until a bed was ready in intensive care.

I asked permission to use the phone and had to keep making calls from the central desk outside Russ's room. I called Russ's mum first. She was planting winter pansies in the garden when his stepfather took the phone out to her. I was too diplomatic, doing such a good job of trying not to alarm her that she asked if she needed to come. I told her she most certainly did, and she left the border half completed as she hurried to get the car ready. I phoned Phil and asked him to contact Eira. Next I rang my parents. My father picked up the phone to hear me begin, 'It's serious, Dad.'

In retrospect, I could have asked someone to ring around but this didn't occur to me at the time. I spoke to Rachel and Lucy on the phone and arranged night cover for them. They seemed happy and enjoying themselves.

'What a relief!' I thought.

Between each call I rushed back to Russ and often had to ring for the nurse, as I could see him deteriorating minute by minute. Once, I said, 'I nearly called the crash team!' and she replied, 'It won't be necessary this time.' Her words shocked me, as it seemed she somehow expected him to deteriorate further. I couldn't believe my ears – and I began to take it in that Russ really was dangerously ill.

Our vicar, Stephen, arrived, with a friend from the lay reader course. I was surprised and relieved that Russ came round sufficiently to remove his oxygen mask and jokingly ask if he was supposed to be preaching on Sunday. He then launched into quoting from the Bible, Romans 5:3,4: 'suffering produces endurance, and endurance produces character, and character produces hope' (RSV). He was certainly my Russ, and I thought how marvellous it was that he knew the Lord and had spent time dwelling on these words from the Bible which were helping him now. Although he said them with a glint in his eye, I knew that he was holding on to them and that his faith was very deep.

Next to arrive at the bedside was Russ's brother, Phil. Russ smiled at him, again managing to find his sense of humour.

'I've obviously not had enough stout!' he quipped.

Russ was my husband but I was painfully aware that he was also the critically ill father of two beautiful daughters, as well as being a brother, son and son-in-law to the people who were dashing to be with him at that moment. I looked out of the window at a tree blowing in the wind. It was getting darker and I wondered what the night would bring.

At last we heard that a bed was available in intensive care. It seemed to take an age for the porters to arrive, and I ran ahead of them, frantically opening doors to make their job easier.

When we reached the lift I rushed up the stairs to avoid causing any delay by squeezing in beside Russ's trolley. But at the top of the stairs, I found myself staring at a closed door to the Intensive Care Unit. The staff gently told me it was best for me to stay outside as they needed to attend to Russ. I felt as though I was pressing against a hard surface, unforgiving, unmovable. I was gutted, desperately yearning to relive the last few minutes. 'Oh, why didn't I go up in the lift with him? Why? Why? Why?' My mind understood what the nurses were saying, but my heart didn't. I felt redundant, discarded, worthless. Russ had been taken from me and I was shut out without any warning. After the sudden shock of leaving home, this was too much. Then I thought, 'Why don't they want me in there? Things must be really bad.'

I started walking listlessly back down the stairs, wondering how long it would be until I saw Russ again, heard him again. I had no idea that never again on this earth would I look into his eyes or hear his voice. Tears

The rest of Russ's family had arrived and I was able to explain a little to them about what would be happening to him – from the knowledge I'd gained on shifts I had done in intensive care. Because of this, the situation seemed more frightening to the others than to me, and I found myself dealing with their emotions and paying less attention to my own. We were shown into a small waiting room; it was quite comfortable and nobody was there apart from us. Staff kept us informed of Russ's progress and told us he was very grateful for the breathing tube which they had passed down his throat to help air get into his lungs.

I knew the anaesthetist was a Christian and that was a great comfort to me. He came and explained, 'Russ has a very severe infection, and even a man with a normal blood count would struggle to fight it. He might pull through, or he might not. We're doing everything we can.'

That was the first real idea I had from an outsider that Russ might even die. It helped tremendously that this man had told me in such a caring way, and I felt reassured that everything possible was being done by the hospital. In the meantime, I kept praying to God and made sure that all our family and some close friends were aware of the severity of the situation. As ever, I believed in the power of prayer in Jesus' name and I desperately wanted people to pray for Russ.

When I was eventually allowed in to see him, I felt quite at home in the surroundings. The unit was in an old part of the hospital, and I've always preferred the 'old' feel to a starchy clinical one. I noticed four or five beds, and Russ was in the second. He was unconscious and his eyes were closed. On his left was a machine recording his heartbeat. I could see bags of fluid on a stand beside him, feeding into his veins through a thin tube. He had a catheter bag too, to make it easier to see how much fluid he was losing. I was familiar with everything about the scene, except that it was my husband in the bed. After reading his charts I sat talking to him even though he made no apparent response – a familiar task, as I'd found myself doing it so often as a nurse.

My parents arrived, my father's arm cradling my mother's shoulder, comforting her as they walked in, and looking at each bed to find us. I smiled weakly and they came over. It didn't occur to me to think of what their journey must have been like, driving the familiar route for two hours but this time knowing it wasn't for a happy family reunion. They asked me to leave them there with him for a while, and I went back to the waiting room.

As the night progressed, I found myself lulled into a false sense of security because Russ's blood pressure was stabilizing in response to the medication. The nurse in charge of his care seemed to agree with my interpretation of this as a positive sign, unwittingly feeding my delusion that he was doing well. I was on a see-saw, one minute thinking he was worse, the next thinking he was better.

Throughout the night I paced up and down beside Russ's bed, praying quietly in a heavenly language. I was just pouring my heart out to God, and it helped me a lot, enabling me to express myself in groanings from deep within and which I knew God understood. His comfort was tangible around and within me, and I prayed for Russ's healing. It was so good to know my brother and his family were wide awake 'across the pond' and I rang them for a few moments so they could pray too.

Around 5.30 a.m. I finished bathing Russ's eyes, and was wondering why the staff did not seem to be as concerned as I was to keep them scrupulously clean. I tried to tell myself that they were letting me do it to keep me occupied, but at the back of my mind I thought, 'They don't think there's any point, they don't want to do anything to distress him. They think he's going to die.'

Then I spotted the catheter bag which had drained only a sparse amount of very dark urine. With horror I saw that it also contained frank blood. I knew then that Russ's kidneys were failing and I felt like a balloon which had just been burst with a needle.

Moment by moment, new and shocking realizations poured into my mind in waves. A different doctor came and sat beside me on a chair a little distance away from the foot of Russ's bed. I hadn't seen him before – he seemed to come out of nowhere. As he spoke about the failure of Russ kidneys and other vital organs, I realized that this doctor was assuming Russ was going to die. In that moment I was oblivious to everything. I felt very alone, removed from normality.

Russ was going to die.

I had gone without sleep all night. I had hardly eaten. And now I had to face the day that my husband would die.

I didn't tell the doctor what was happening to me, but let him assume that I knew already that Russ was dying, even though I hadn't known until that moment. I felt as though I'd just fallen off a cliff onto the rocks below. I don't know how long I sat there after I saw the doctor. A nurse brought me a cup of tea and I noticed listlessly that dawn was breaking.

As I drank the tea I plucked up courage to go and tell Russ's family what was happening. Nothing could have been more awful. We were all in shock and everything seemed completely unreal – none of us could take in that this was really happening. His mother, Sybil, looked straight ahead, dazed, and then looked at me with such love in her eyes.

I said, 'We still don't know for sure what's going to happen, but we do know lots of people are praying.' I sensed their relief as I said it. We were all living from moment to moment, desperate for any news, however small. Every one of us was floundering in this stretch of stormy sea, each individual swimming against the tide, alone in our private battles, but aware that we were in it together.

I don't think I cried at that time. I was thinking about everyone else, and how they felt. After twenty minutes I got up and walked along the corridor to the two large doors of the Intensive Care Unit. Breathing deeply to steady myself, I pushed them open and stepped inside. Russ looked just the same, lying there, calm, seemingly unaware I had returned. But while I bathed his eyes I carried on talking to him and every moment I felt the great weight in the pit of my stomach getting heavier.

It was then I began to think what I would say to the girls. Winston's Wish is the leading childhood bereavement charity in the UK, and I remembered meeting the founder, Julie Stokes, when I nursed at the Sue Ryder hospice. We had chatted by the lake as she visited her very first family as founder of that organization.

Now when I picked up the phone I said, 'I'd like some help, please.' Then I paused, trying to find the words. Saying them out loud would make them terrifyingly real. 'I need to know how to tell my young children that their daddy will probably die today.'

A lovely woman was at the other end. She listened for as long as I wanted to talk and gave me valuable advice on how to break the news to the girls, suggesting I recount the events of the previous day leading up to the present situation.

Soon afterwards, the staff told me the girls were outside. This was the most heartrending part of all for me. I walked towards the doors and went out to them. Rachel and Lucy were with Jackie, and after a brief word she slipped away, into a side room. The three of us were alone in a bare corridor in the old building. As I spoke, Rachel looked away and then took her pencil and writing pad out of her bag and began to draw, her young mind trying to make sense of what she was hearing. Lucy burst into tears.

I don't know how I got through that moment. It chokes me now to think about it. This was probably the worst moment of my life, and I asked God to prevent me ever having to do something like it again. Time seemed to have stopped and I was facing a brick wall.

After a few minutes, I asked the girls if they wanted to go in to see Daddy. They were used to hospitals by now and I explained that although he couldn't speak, he could probably hear them and would know they were there. I described what he would look like. Taking their small hands in mine, we went into intensive care.

The girls walked slowly up to Russ while I talked to them all the time. Their eyes were wide open, taking in their new surroundings. We moved the table to make a space for them to squeeze in beside him.

'Can he see me at all, Mummy?' Rachel whispered.

'I don't think so, darling, but I think he knows you're here and he's really pleased.' Rachel was quiet after that and rested her paper on a table and drew. Lucy sat on my lap, watching him. We went back to the waiting family about fifteen minutes later. It was early morning and my parents had just returned from a few hours in a local hotel – now they went in to spend time with Russ. Russ's whole family had stayed in the little waiting room all this time, taking it in turns to go and sit with Russ, except for Sybil who couldn't bring herself to go in yet.

'Are you angry, Mum?' Eira asked her.

'No, I'm just very sorry,' Sybil answered.

The girls and I went back into Russ's room, and after ten minutes Rachel looked up at me and said, 'I want to go home.'

'Of course, darling. Jackie will take you,' I replied.

Jackie had been a Godsend, looking after the children while I was at the hospital. I felt confident that she could handle this tough development. But Rachel insisted, 'No, Mummy, I want you to take me home.' I looked at Russ and then at Rachel and Lucy. I knew that my place was now with them, and I knew something else too – with complete confidence, I knew that Russ was all right.

The children kissed their daddy and told him they loved him. They went out to get ready while I stayed for a moment to say goodbye. I stroked his head, noticing that, like Samson in the Bible, his hair was starting to grow again. I kissed him and held him and whispered, 'Thank you, darling, for being such a wonderful husband to me and such a loving, perfect father to the girls. We have been so happy, and we have known such love. Thank you.'

Then I forced myself to get up from beside the bed. As I walked to the door, I turned to take my last look at him, and in that moment I saw Jesus, not physically but in a spiritual sense. I knew, as surely as I know that I am Judy Hopkins, that I was leaving Russ in the care of Christ. I had no concern that he would be alone at the moment of death. Neither was I alone, for our God was taking care of us all. Then I deliberately turned away from Russ, the husband I loved so dearly, and walked into the future with our girls.

We had been home for about an hour when the hospital rang and I knew immediately that they were about to tell me Russ had died. When I left, the staff had really thought he would survive until later in the day, and had said I should have plenty of time to return to see him. But I'd walked out of the hospital feeling certain I would never see my husband alive here on earth again.

With an utter emptiness inside me I went back to Russ's bedside. Because I had nursed so many dying people, the surroundings all seemed quite familiar. Except this time, it was Russ. I was struck by a sense of tremendous peace. I could feel God's presence with me, as though I were enveloped in a soft velvetiness. I was stunned to see the radiant smile on Russ's face and wondered if this was due to the intubation tube, but as I took his hand, I saw that he really was radiant. I now had no doubt that he was with the Lord; his body left like a discarded coat on the hospital bed. I could hardly bear to tear myself away from the place – I could have stayed there for hours.

My one regret was that I'd let the girls go to town with Jackie. I remember she bought them each a toy puppy with a bottle, and they kept those puppies for a long time. Before leaving home, I'd told them very gently that their daddy had now died. The hospital staff reassured me that Russ should look much the same at the funeral directors, but in fact his expression had dulled when we saw him there. It's an even bigger reason to cherish the touch of heaven I experienced in that hospital room.

There was nothing left to say or do. Mum and Dad drove me home from the hospital. My mind was in a state of shock and denial. I whispered to my father, 'This is a dream, isn't it? Tell me it's a dream.'

With tears in his eyes he replied slowly, 'No, Judy, I'm afraid it isn't.'

14

BLUR AND HOPE

I remember almost nothing of the evening after Russ died. I know I got home in the afternoon and my parents stayed awhile, and that I spoke to my sister-in-law on the phone. She began, 'Hello, Judy. How is . . .'

'He's gone, Jackie,' was all I managed.

Friends from church rallied round to sort out care for the girls, and for someone to be with me. After my parents left in the evening, a friend, Jackie, came over. Russ and I had shared many laughs with her, and I was really grateful to her husband for not minding when she stayed overnight. She listened while I talked about the way Russ had died – going over and over what I could have done differently. It was 1.00 a.m. when my head finally hit the pillow of the new double bed.

After an hour I woke with a start, 'Russ has died!' The realization hit me like a bolt. I had to get out of my room, had to walk, had to do something. I rushed downstairs and found Jackie lying on the sofa.

'He's dead, Jackie. I can't believe it,' I cried out.

Then I crouched over in front of the patio doors saying, 'My stomach, my stomach! It's hurting, Jackie. It's hurting!' I did cry but it was mostly the physical pain I was aware of. After a while she led me to the sofa and held me for a long, long time.

Eventually she said, 'Come on, Judy, I'll get your duvet and you can sleep down here.'

We spent the rest of the night sleeping top to tail on the sofa. She said it rained, very loudly, on the sloping roof.

The rest of that week is a blur. I do remember registering the death. My father drove me into Cheltenham to the modern office building and his love and business expertise got me through. The female registrar recognized me from before my marriage when I had nursed one of her relatives. I felt that God was affirming me as an individual apart from my husband, with an identity and history of my own in Cheltenham. I remembered Russ's words to me as we left Bristol: 'It's important for you that I get you away from here now.' It was becoming quite special to me that he'd felt compelled to uproot me from Bristol and plant me back home in Cheltenham before the end came.

Immediately after Russ's death I didn't want any flowers, and certainly didn't want a service. But then the first arrangement arrived, and I was so comforted by the scent, the beauty of the flowers, and the card with loving words. Within two days I felt ready to prepare the service.

As we'd discussed, I took Rachel and Lucy to the funeral directors to see their daddy's body. First I explained how he would look, and I was very careful not to force them or even suggest that they should go. Both nodded that they still wanted to. Again I had adult support – my friend and trainee minister, Val, drove us there, and she was a huge source of strength to me as we walked into the chapel of rest. Russ's body lay in the room, which I had intended to fill with flowers for their scent, but I hadn't managed it.

His face didn't have the same radiance as in the hospital room, but nevertheless, the girls walked straight up to him. They sat next to him and then danced around in the room. They were so at ease that when Bob, a lay reader from church, called, Rachel grabbed him in the corridor, begging, 'Come and see my daddy!'

I don't think Bob quite knew what to say. He had been a comedian in his younger days and wasn't usually lost for words. I smiled to myself, knowing how Russ would have laughed, seeing the amusing side of it.

After an hour or so, we all prayed, and left. Gently I told the children that they would not see their daddy's body again. I reassured them he was alive in heaven and would have a new body there. I could tell them this because I believed God's word with all my heart; for me it was not an empty hope but a certain one.

A day or so later, my friend Linda arrived, and we began a significant period of supporting each other, usually over the phone, which was to continue for the coming months and years. She's a skilled musician and advised me on the suitability of the songs and hymns I had chosen. Now I had accepted there would be a service, I decided it would be one of thanksgiving for Russ's life. as I made the funerals I conducted

Linda's support is an example of how different friends had specific roles at this time. It seemed that God was blending them all together to forge a solid network for me. Our vicar, Stephen, was also a great support and sat with us at home planning the service.

I knew that it is quite usual for the bereaved person to find an extra source of strength in the very early days of grief. That's what happened to me. I found I was able to manage and organize all the things that needed doing. I

* So sad that I had no grief, simply gratitude to God for ending suffering for us both.

placed a notification of Russ's death in the local papers and added at the bottom, 'He loved Jesus'. I might phrase it differently now, but the meaning would be the same, because Russ did love Jesus.

The thanksgiving service was arranged for Friday, and by Thursday our home was full. Russ's family had arrived and mine had travelled from as far afield as Boston, USA. I managed to escape upstairs for an hour to prepare a tribute to Russ and was grateful for a time of peace, and the chance to put pen to paper. It was amazing how easily the words flowed. My sister Jackie helped me edit, and Eira typed. Meanwhile, a friend called in with a wonderful enlarged print of Russ from a photo taken on our honeymoon. My father had been astounded at how calmly and easily I had found the original amongst a jumble of negatives tucked in an old bag in the garage. He often mentioned it afterwards, particularly when he saw it hanging in Lucy's bedroom.

On Friday morning, 3 November 2000, I picked out two contrasting outfits, knowing all the time which one I would choose – and my mum knew, too. I rejected the dark skirt and top, and slipped on the Laura Ashley dress which I'd first worn a few months earlier when Russ and I went for our final meal out together. It was yellow with beautiful embroidery running down the fabric of the skirt. To me it symbolized life. It was the right dress.

Shortly before the service, our families arrived at our house from their overnight accommodation. Two years earlier, many of us had met in our home before Phil's wedding. I flinched at the contrast now.

We waited quietly for the car to arrive and were driven along the familiar route where Russ had driven us every Sunday morning. But today was Friday.

'Oh, why isn't it Sunday?' I cried out inside. 'Why can't I blink my eyes and everything be as it was? What's happening? How can Russ have died?'

The girls interrupted my thoughts. They needed me. They hadn't taken in what was happening either; their Daddy's death hadn't sunk in. As Russ was a working father they had always relied on me most, and even since his hospitalization he had been in and out of their daily routine. We arrived at our church, the girls each clutching a letter and a toy for daddy. Lucy had chosen a dinosaur, and Rachel, a beanie lobster. We walked to the front, and they placed them on top of the coffin where their father's body lay.

The church was packed with people from all walks of Russ's life; a few had not really known him, but had come to support me. I sat in the front with my brother by my side. He was such a support. Our vicar conducted a very special service, and our best man, Nick, spoke of his friendship with Russ. The Winchcombe Town Band, where Russ had been a member for fourteen years, played the hymn he loved so much, 'Amazing Grace' by John Newton. I was proud to give a tribute to Russ and used a bar of chocolate, a Bible and some climbing ropes to illustrate some of the things he'd loved.

At the end of the service, the family filed out while two friends sang 'Jesus Shall Take the Highest Honour' by Chris Bowater, a chorus Russ and I had chosen for our wedding. When the song ended, the silence was broken by a lone voice from the congregation taking up the chorus again. One by one, individuals joined in until everyone was on their feet, singing. God's Holy Spirit was truly moving in that place, and touching people's hearts. One of Russ's work colleagues later remarked that she had never experienced anything like it. As a funeral should be. After John Greenwood funeral someone thanked me, saying they had never been to a funeral laughed - even his widow + daughters were laughing I'm sure he was too!

Rachel and Lucy stayed for most of the service, before going out to the hall to play with the toys. They were used to the church building, so it was very comfortable and familiar to them. Two friends took care of them while I went to the crematorium with the rest of the family. The girls didn't want to come, and that was fine. They were playing happily, as they would do after a Sunday service, though aware that this one was different from usual.

By prior arrangement, a song written by Jim Cowan and sung by Robin Mark was played at the crematorium service. I had happened to listen to it for the first time the previous day. It speaks of a life lived for Christ and, like the dress, I knew it was right.

> When it's all been said and done
> There is just one thing that matters -
> Did I do my best to live for truth?
> Did I live my life for you?
>
> All my treasures will mean nothing,
> Only what I've done for love's reward
> Will stand the test of time.
> *Jim Cowan © 1999 Integrity's Hosanna!*

After the cremation we drove to the church hall for the tea. As the car got closer, my mouth got drier.

Dad placed his hand on mine. 'It'll soon be over, darling.' My brother nodded and then firmly but gently placed his hand on my shoulder. I felt a little bit of confidence rising in me.

We arrived. I reached the hall door and stopped to lift my head and silently pray, 'Help me, God.' Then I went in. The layout of the room helped, as I was able to slip in at one end without everyone noticing. I looked around at the sea of faces, feeling strangely warmed. I spoke with Russ's work colleagues, friends and family, including his stepfather's family who had come over from Holland. It was comforting to speak with the two nurses who had been particularly involved in caring for Russ in Bristol. I discovered, too, that when I'd left the hospital, Sybil had gone into his room, with Eira. I was really pleased for them, that they'd been there when he died.

I left about two hours later, clutching a list of everyone who had come to the service, including those who had not been at the tea. I felt very touched that someone had organized this for me.

When we arrived home, I slipped outside almost immediately and sat in our car. I played a favourite CD, turning the volume up high. Overwhelmed by the lyrics, I got out and knelt on the patch of grass in front of our house, oblivious to anyone and everything around me. At the deepest level I felt death permeating my heart and understanding. I could feel the person I'd chosen to spend my life with being wrenched apart from me and, in a pain more agonizing than I'd ever experienced before, I cried out to my heavenly Father.

That night and all the next day my sister, Jackie, spent a lot of time listening as I talked through the details of Russ's death. She has said since, 'You seemed in a daze, Judy, stopping every now and then in the middle of a sentence to stare out the window.'

I read every card out to her and took immense comfort from each one.

It meant a lot to me to have my teenage nephew and niece with me at this time, even though I felt a little disgruntled when they understandably needed attention from Jackie. I was mainly focused on myself. I said I didn't mind the TV on, but it seemed so removed from what I was going through and like an intrusion from another world.

The rest of my family stayed for a few days and we went out once for a meal. Although I wanted to sit with my brother and his family, Rachel and Lucy spotted a cozy little table in the corner and begged me to sit with them there. I reluctantly agreed, knowing they wanted me to themselves. I needed to be there for them, but it was a lonely place for me to be.

Just as they were leaving, my father beckoned to me. 'Now, the next few weeks are going to be particularly hard, Judy. I suggest that at 6 o'clock every day, you check that you've eaten, or at least that you're going to eat. I know you'll look after the girls, but you must look after yourself. Promise me.'

I promised.

Suddenly, finally, everyone had gone. The three of us were alone together. We had no idea what the future would bring. I clung to the fact that God did know, and we were in his hands. He had promised he would never leave us, so we didn't have to face the future alone.

Three days later, Lucy nestled into my bed and prayerfully said sorry for anything she had done wrong and that she believed in and wanted to follow Jesus. This was completely unprompted by me, and she continues to remember it, even recalling the blue silk dress she was wearing. Rachel had already prayed a similar prayer, so as a family we were trusting in his direction. Soon after this, a friend told me that while she had been praying for us, she 'saw' Rachel holding Jesus' right hand and Lucy holding his left. It was a wonderful picture, confirming what others had said to me – that God would look after my girls. I felt sure they were going to be all right.

15

EARLY DAYS

In the early days after the thanksgiving service, a great deal of my grieving was focused on the medical details and wondering whether anything could have been done to prevent Russ's death. Could I have done anything? Could the hospital have done something differently? These questions went round and round in my mind. And I had no answers then.

During the first week after Russ died, Phil and I went to Bristol to discuss the details leading to Russ's discharge with the consultant. We had both heard him tell Russ he could be discharged, and I needed to hear him explain why. Now he told us that when he'd seen Russ, he'd assessed that he was definitely ready to be discharged and treated as an outpatient. He reiterated what the registrar had told us, that Russ's blood results indicated he was able to be at home, and that in many cases it was the safest place for a transplant patient at Russ's stage. He told me that Russ's infection could well have proved fatal even if he was still in hospital at Bristol, and I realized there was always a danger he could have got an infection through staying there. The consultant looked at me directly and said, 'People die here too, Judy.'

Phil and I returned to Cheltenham satisfied with his answers.

I also needed to approach the consultant in Cheltenham hospital, where Russ had spent his last twenty-four hours, and I was terrified of finding that something could have been done to save him. But that question was far too painful to address yet, even though I knew that one day I would make the visit, and face what was now unthinkable. I remember Mum asking me, 'Why must you do all this, Judy? Russ has died, and we can't bring him back.'

'I know, Mum. I just have to understand what happened so I can make sense of it in my mind.'

A few weeks later I returned to Bristol to see the consultant again, and this time I asked my friend Gail to come with me. I'd had time to mull over some of the medical facts and needed further reassurance and clarification. Gail and I had been colleagues at the Sue Ryder hospice, and I felt she was the right person to support me over the medical details. I told the hospital staff how grateful I was, stressing that I had come to have some questions answered, and not to criticize.

The consultant was very approachable.

'I was very surprised to hear that Russ had died,' he told me, 'although I shouldn't have been.' I knew he had been straight with us right from the beginning. 'I told you that a transplant for Russ was a risk. Recovery is never certain. Even if he had recovered, there was a strong chance that his leukaemia would have returned.' I also understood him to say that even if we had known Russ's diagnosis earlier, with his condition he would still have needed the transplant, and would probably have had a graft-versus-host reaction.

The consultant had been away on the day of Russ's discharge from Bristol, and a female registrar there had spoken to me on the phone on the evening of his death. With the blood results in front of her, she had told me there was absolutely no reason why Russ should not have been discharged from Bristol. She'd been tremendously kind and had reassured me that I had done nothing wrong; it had been their decision, which the consultant reiterated. In my heart I still sensed a need to forgive her for sending him home, even though she had done nothing wrong. It was to take some months before I found that peace. I understand this.

Gail and I went on to visit the registrar who had spoken of feeling privileged to operate on my husband when the Hickman line in his chest had become infected. I thanked him for all he'd done, giving him a copy of the tribute I had paid to Russ at the Service of Thanksgiving. He said he would never forget my husband.

A few days later, I visited Russ's workplace. I'd planned to leave Lucy in the car with a friend, but she had other ideas and desperately wanted to come inside. I decided to take her in and a lovely woman on reception took charge of her for me. I had only ever been as far as the entrance to Russ's office, and now found it profoundly moving to sit at his double desk. It was still known as *Russ's desk* although someone else was using it now.

Many of Russ's colleagues had developed a real respect for him in the short time he had been there; most were of a similar age and had been deeply affected by his death. I was very touched when the manager withdrew from an important meeting to spend time with me. He and Russ's immediate boss both wanted to help in any way they could, and I very much appreciated their love and concern. As I left the office, the staff invited me to visit any time. Russ's employer said, 'You're very much part of our work family, as Russ was,' and I appreciated those words so much. It was then I noticed a very happy Lucy in reception. Not only did I find out later that she had brought sunshine into the office that day, but I also discovered that her name means 'light bringer'. I had walked into an atmosphere of sadness, yet Lucy had brought joy.

There was a job I needed to face. I sat and wrote a letter of forgiveness to all the people responsible for him being discharged. I never intended to send it, but experienced a tremendous release of emotions as I wrote. Then I burned the letter and asked God to forgive me if I had let Russ down in any way through things I had done or failed to do. I knew that – despite my flaws and faults – undeserved grace and love flow continuously from the heart of God. As I prayed about this, I remembered Russ telling me that God had told him, 'I am in charge of your life.'

As well as Russ's workplace, my other early visit was to Harnhill Centre for Christian Healing where I wanted to speak about the vision Russ had before he died. This is a beautifully appointed country manor near Cirencester, where many people come to hear speakers, to mingle and pray. One couple there had prayerfully supported me throughout Russ's illness. During my visit, I shared with them some glimpses of our experience of God's presence through our terrible ordeal.

On my way out, it struck me that although I'd shared many things that day, I hadn't sensed God speaking to me personally. Without knowing why, and even though my car was parked at the front of the centre, I turned around and walked towards the back of the house. As I approached the door, I lifted my eyes and saw an inscription from the Bible: 'I am the resurrection and the life. He who believes in me will live, even though he dies; and whoever lives and believes in me will never die' (John 11:25,26).

My heart thumped with the powerful realization that Jesus himself was using that moment to speak to me personally. With utter conviction I knew that my Redeemer lived, and I was certain that Russ was alive with him.

A s I KNOW my loved ones are, especially Daddy, Bryan + Richard Stannett.

16

GLIMPSES OF REALITY

Slowly, gradually, the weeks passed. I wrote in my journal, 'The pain seems more acute than ever and impossible to put into words.'

Early one morning I drove the girls to a little park in Charlton Kings, near to the spot where I'd collected Russ from work every day. Rachel was pushing Lucy on the swing while I watched, and they were framed by several trees half stripped of their summer foliage. A leaf fluttered down beside me. I knelt on the ground and prayed, 'God, I can't do this alone. You must help me. Please, please send the girls another father.'

There was silence. And then, 'Mummy, push me! Mummy! Want to go higher, Mummy!' It was Lucy. So I got up – and pushed her higher.

We spent the fourth weekend with my parents in Wellingborough, and on the Sunday I decided to accompany my father to the early morning service at his church. It was the place where Russ and I had been married. Sitting in the car waiting for my dad, I mulled over the bleakness of my situation. I was still in shock, struggling with every fibre of my being to accept the monumental change in my life and comprehend the prospect of bringing up our daughters alone. I felt inconsolable.

All of a sudden, a hymn on the radio caught my attention, 'Because He lives', with the lyrics including the line that we can face tomorrow because of Jesus. That was it. Hope surged through my being. I could face tomorrow because Jesus Christ was real and alive. My life was committed to him; he was my rock, my reason for living, and he would help me with the girls.

In church during the service, my eyes were drawn to a picture of Jesus holding a sheep, and with two lambs at his feet. Although I had grown up as a member of that church, I'd never taken much notice of the picture before. Now as I gazed at it, I knew the girls and I would be looked after by the great Shepherd of the sheep. When I was least expecting it, God had spoken to me and poured his strength into my aching heart.

On Thursday I ticked off another week on the calendar since Russ had died. It would be a whole year before I would forget precisely how many weeks had passed and progress to counting in months and finally, as time elapsed, to years.

Bereavement brings a mountain of paperwork along with it. This had to be fitted around caring for the girls – who took up most of my time – but a friend from a nearby church, whose mother I had nursed, advised me on social service issues. While my finances were being processed, I signed on at social security. (Later I was able to pay back the funds from my widowed mother's allowance.) As I first sat in the stark benefits office waiting room with Rachel and Lucy, my eyes filled with tears as I remembered Russ striding eagerly into the next-door office three years earlier to register Lucy's birth.

There were numerous visits to the tax office, again taking one or both of the girls with me. It was a struggle to make sure I had photocopied all the necessary documents, and at every visit I found myself having to explain yet again that my husband had died. After hearing a few words of sympathy I was then required to give intimate details of our finances and income. These experiences left me feeling raw.

I had to surrender Russ's endowment mortgage and activate a few small pensions. I then began navigating my way through the red tape surrounding widows' allowances and legal affairs – we hadn't made a will. All this was a hard, complex but unavoidable part of the process.

People wrote me lovely letters, all of which are very precious to me, particularly those which mentioned Russ. One work colleague even enclosed a printout of some joke instructions written by Russ to anyone using his PC while he was in hospital.

During the approach to Christmas I visited Russ's colleagues at his old and new workplaces; they were very gracious. I went because I needed to. After twelve years of knowing him, and eight and a half of seeing him every day, it was taking time for me to get used to his physical absence, and to the abrupt change in our daily routine. By the following year I would visit just to take them all a cake, and by the fourth Christmas I actually forgot to go. The process of recovery felt like being a pendulum on a big clock, first clicking forcefully from side to side, then after driving the hands many times around the clock face, gradually coming to rest.

The pendulum was swinging fast that first Christmas, but I found the holiday easier than many people had imagined. It was two months since Russ had died and I had begun a nightly ritual of falling into bed, completely exhausted after seeing to the girls. I would read myself to sleep with a Christian biography of someone in a similar

situation to mine, which would always give me comfort.
The first I read was *Rainbows through the Rain,* written by
Fiona Castle after her husband Roy died of cancer in
1994. I later read another of her books, *No Flowers, Just
Lots of Joy,* and found many similarities between our
experiences, particularly in the way our husbands had
handled their illnesses. Of course, Fiona's was a much
more public journey than mine, but God used her memories to encourage me tremendously in those early days.

At the end of the school term, the children had their
nativity play. Because I couldn't face going alone, my
sister-in-law, Anne, came along with me. My eyes kept
filling with tears as I watched our girls play their parts,
and I longed for Russ to be there too. Gradually I built
up a list of two or three friends who would accompany
me on these occasions – the times when Russ and I
would have gone together. I managed the end of term
'looking at books' session by myself. Parents gathered in
the classroom as their children proudly displayed their
work. Few of them realized how very painful these
events were for me and, of course, most were busy looking at their children's work. I was proud of my girls, but
ached and yearned to have their father with me to share
their achievements. I missed my husband – and cried
out to myself, 'Oh, why isn't he by my side?'

At Christmas I kept to our tradition of going to stay
with my parents. Mum and I both expected laughter as
well as tears. As usual there were lots of guests to cater
for, and although we knew it would be tough, we
thought Russ's absence might seem easier to handle that
way than it would have done in a small family gathering. After Christmas lunch, I managed to escape for a
quiet walk. As I reached a bend in the country lane, I
paused to gaze at the field where I had sledged as a
child. I stood, tears streaming down my cheeks. And

then at that moment, I believe I heard God. I sensed him impressing on me that he would reveal his glory through the girls and me as we moved forward and trusted him. It was as if a picture formed in my mind of a beacon on a hill giving light, and a tremendous peace descended on me. Two years later, a woman told me that while she was praying for our family, she had seen a picture of a beacon on a hill.

I walked back to the house to rejoin the others, relieved the day was almost over. I was particularly helped that first Christmas by those who let me talk about Russ. Several people in their twenties and thirties seemed to understand that too much superficial small talk can be frustrating when you're dealing with life on a deeper level. When you're facing pain and loss you don't want others to gloss over it, and it helped enormously to be allowed to be real in front of them. It reminded me of when my grandfather had died, and my mother said that not to speak of him was like a denial of his life. YES

The girls and I celebrated New Year with Jackie and her husband Jerry in their country home, along with twenty of their family and friends. At midnight I went to my room to be quiet, but came back downstairs later and chatted to a guest. As I shared part of my story with her, silly woman she asked, 'Don't you think the hospital was negligent in some way, Judy?' This set a stream of unhelpful thoughts racing to the front of my mind. I was coming to discover in my grief that some questions can seem all-consuming. They would fade as I wrestled with them, only to rear their head again later if I hadn't dealt with them fully. This question of negligence hadn't been resolved in my mind, and I still tortured myself with the feeling that somehow I could have altered the outcome. Was I in some way responsible for my girls having lost their father?

The return journey home on 2 January 2001 was the hardest part of Christmas for me. I was in turmoil, facing the harsh reality that my family had been torn apart. The girls and I had been away for ten days and were now coming back to a cold and empty house. I could hardly bear the pain as I unloaded the car; memories of our old routine threatened to overwhelm me. Whenever we had got home from a journey, I would go in and settle the girls, while Russ unpacked the car. Tears of pain mingled with disbelief rolled down my cheeks, and I cried out to God for help. Minutes later, it came in the form of a phone call.

'It's Yvonne here. Can I come and see you? There's something I want to show you.'

'Of course,' I replied, frantically trying to remember who Yvonne was and wondering how to give her directions when I had no idea where she lived. After asking a few questions, I realized that Yvonne had been on the lay reader training course with Russ. She arrived within the hour, cradling two lovely plants which were a gift for me from the lay readers on the course. Tucked in her bag was a piece of paper, the real reason for her visit. I made us a drink, and she began to share her story of the day Russ had died.

> That day was my birthday, and because I knew Russ's condition was very serious, I went into Gloucester Cathedral to pray for him. Unbeknown to me, I was actually there during the time that Russ died. *God-incidence*
>
> I was feeling so down and devastated by the news of Russ's worsening situation, and it looked as if we were going to lose him. Because it was my birthday, it seemed that little bit worse. I just couldn't settle at all. So I went into the cathedral and sat in my favourite chapel, where Thomas Denny has his blue windows.

There was scaffolding outside and so the windows seemed very dark. That was fine, and it suited my mood. I spent some time just praying, really asking God why this was happening and if anything could be done. I asked him if Russ could please be spared to live, and for my prayer to make all the difference.

Then I put my elbows on the arm of the chair. My eyes were closed, but when I opened them I could see a surprising reflection in the stones of my engagement ring, as I was holding my hand in front of my face. I had never seen any kind of reflection like it before.

I could see one of the smaller windows reflected in my ring. The window had a splash of yellow in it that brightened the whole thing up.

It seemed to me as if God was saying to me that Russ was above all earthly doubts now, above all the need for reassurance, and that he was safe. At the same time a chorus came into my mind, 'Behold the Lamb', and I just knew that that was what Russ was doing. Right then.

It was as if God wanted us to know that Russ's place was with him in heaven. He was above earthly cares, above earthly things, he was with God and he would be happy, and for Russ the chorus line 'Behold the Lamb' was happening in reality.

As soon as she finished speaking, Yvonne placed her hand on my shoulder, looked into my eyes and said, 'Judy, you did nothing wrong.' That perfectly timed reassurance settled me more than I can say. And the picture she shared spoke to my inner being. I didn't know why Russ had died, but I had the assurance that God did. I believed with all my heart that Russ was beholding the Lamb, Jesus himself.

Yvonne had kept that story to herself for two months. She knew nothing of my movements over Christmas, but that day, 2 January, she sensed that God wanted her to tell me what had happened. She was obedient and I was truly blessed.

She stressed how God was my rock, a truth which was repeated in cards from many other friends. After her visit, I experienced a tremendous peace which lasted five days. But on Saturday 6 January 2001 the peace was replaced by desolation. Quite suddenly, for the first time since that Friday evening seven months earlier when the doctor had brought the news of Russ's illness, I lost the tangible sense of the presence of God. I was in despair, agony; all my feelings were jagged and raw, rubbing and jarring inside of me. Gradually I began to wonder whether this was an extreme example of a method God might be using to peel away a layer of grief. Was he allowing my pain to reach a point of eruption where a burst of grief would well up and overflow? After this first time, the pattern was to continue over the next four years with variable intensity, each time lasting up to a few days. As the pain reached a peak it was as unbearable as food poisoning or labour contractions, and then gradually wore off. Once I'd recognized the pattern, I was able to cope better with the pain because I knew progress was being made and relief would come. But on this first occasion I just sobbed my heart out to a friend over the phone.

The next day, as I stood in church singing the hymn, 'Lord for the Years' by Timothy Dudley-Smith, my mind went back to the times when I had sung it with Russ in St Paul's, and most recently at a wedding we'd attended just before his transplant. I was deeply impacted by the words of the last verse

> Lord for ourselves; in living power remake us -
> Self on the cross and Christ upon the throne,
> Past put behind us, for the future take us;

YES
Sides
892

yes - this means so much to me .
He did this for me on 29.820 - a whole new life
began

Lord of our lives, to live for Christ alone.[2]

As the hymn ended, a friend placed her hand on me and I felt myself gently sink down to the floor, only aware of a sea of faces gathering above me. There was a real crying from deep within me, and I knew that God's Holy Spirit had truly touched me.

That evening, for the first time since losing him, I could look at Russ's picture without feeling pain. Tears were still flowing, but inside I felt the beginning of contentment. A few days later I likened my feelings to being on a train. God was driving, and there was no need for me to get on or off – I just had to sit there. Another helpful analogy came into my mind, that it was as if my life were a tour of the British Isles. Russ and I had journeyed together for a season, but I still had some travelling to do without him. *I used this concept to a widow – that her husband had just gone on ahead of her*

Time meandered slowly and pretty much without purpose. During January I made several trips up Cleeve Hill, reliving my last walk with Russ.

One day as I was rifling through a cupboard at home for something I'd lost, I cried out in desperation to God, 'How am I going to manage, Lord?' He seemed to answer me by bringing back the memory of a previous experience in Uganda in 1990. During my two month visit to my missionary friend, Margaret, I had made an excursion to see Rwandan gorillas. Several of us had clambered through dense undergrowth to track them down, depending totally on our guide, because we had no idea how to find the path ahead. I believe God brought this memory into my mind to illustrate that he was now my guide for the way ahead. I didn't know the path, but my part was just to follow and trust his leading.

There was an evening when I took Lucy and Rachel back to Radio Lollipop in Bristol with Jackie's children, who they had stayed with when Russ was in Bristol. The girls loved showing them the room where they had played so many times. Rachel cheerfully told them about the day she had made patient wrist labels for Lucy and herself and then persuaded the volunteers to escort them back to a ward, pretending they were patients! It gave me real pleasure to reinforce these happy memories of Bristol with the girls. Although the return journey was really tough without Russ, we still ended up singing. It had been right to go.

In February my parents had a pre-planned holiday in Tenerife, and they were really keen for us to join them. We had been with them before Russ died and it meant so much to my parents and the girls that I agreed to go. In all honesty, I would have preferred to stay in the familiar surroundings of the home in which Russ and I had invested so much of our hearts. Somehow I felt safe and close to him there, with people around me who knew and loved him. We had a kind offer of a lift to and from the airport; it was reassuring to have that support because I was feeling so vulnerable and weighed down with responsibility.

As we checked through customs, I leafed through the passports and found myself opening Russ's passport to gaze at him. It would be three more years before I felt ready to leave his passport behind when we travelled as a family. As we searched for our cases in the baggage arrival hall in Tenerife, the memory of Russ laying Lucy in the top section of the luggage trolley as a baby flooded my mind.

The holiday proved to be even tougher than I'd anticipated. We stayed in my parents' timeshare apartment and did many of the things I'd done before with Russ. Although I had to face the same pain and memories every day at home, being plunged back into this holiday scenario was almost too hard to bear. Mum and Dad were very kind and I'm sure the experience was good for us as a family, but I found it excruciatingly painful to follow a routine where everything was the same except that Russ was missing.

When I got into bed on the last night of the holiday I prayed to be given a dream about him. The dream that came has never left me. We were all at home in my dining room. While my parents chatted and the girls played, I suddenly realized that Russ was there with us. He put his right arm around my shoulder and his left hand beneath my neck, and gently drew me away to a corner of the room. I prodded his arm and exclaimed, 'But . . . you're real!' He replied, with a knowing chuckle, 'Oh yes, I'm real.' I touched him again. Yes! He was so real! Then he took me and cradled me in his arms. His embrace conveyed a depth and purity that far transcended his nature on earth.

The comfort of that embrace – which had been so real and tangible – lingered on in my mind and heart for many months. When we got home from Tenerife, I received a letter emphasizing that God was holding me particularly close at this time. There was also a phone message from a friend urging me to look up a Bible verse – Song of Songs 2:6: 'His left arm is under my head'. Again I felt a sure confirmation of God's love and care for me. I didn't need to speculate about the details of the dream. I just accepted that it was from God, and that Russ was very much alive with him. That was enough.

17

KNOTS AND TEARS

The early stages of my grieving were coloured by my past experiences. I had known the deaths of grandparents and various aunts and uncles, but these had seemed timely and I'd felt fairly removed from them. As a nurse I'd studied the process of death professionally and had also nursed the dying: but now I was experiencing these things at first-hand.

Slowly I began to see that grief is a process, a meandering stream that needs to run its course. A moving mass, thrusting in one direction and then lunging back, often covering the same ground until it is able to move on. I was finding the process exhausting, requiring tremendous inner resources to get through, and with little to show for much of the journey. I remembered some words I had read by Nikos Kazantzakis, when he watched a butterfly preparing to emerge from its cocoon. It was taking too long for Nikos, so he bent over and breathed out to warm it. In wonder he saw the butterfly emerge – but then his heart sank to see her wings folded back and crumpled. A few seconds later, she died. He had tried to hurry this natural process.

I wanted my grief to find its fullest expression, by avoiding burying things deep within me in case they festered and caused pain later. So I expressed my pain, my questions, and my unforgiveness.

good

I kept going for my daughters' sake, but I knew I'd put a lot of my personal grief on hold. I couldn't protect myself from the shock of Russ's death and that had to be absorbed somehow, but I began to see it was going to take time to be released and healed.

Sometimes my mind sped into such deep turmoil that it frightened me. Then I was given a really helpful poem from the childhood bereavement charity Winston's Wish called 'That's Normal', which I kept stuck on my fridge. It said that if you thought you were going insane, that was normal. That helped me to understand that it's natural to feel turmoil during times of grief, and that when the feeling persists and affects your life outwardly, you need help to process what's going on. I found it best to focus on one practical thing at a time and get through the day, or just the next hour. At times even that was tremendously difficult.

At the lowest times I would invariably end up talking to a friend, who would patiently listen while my thoughts began to untangle. As a child I was keen on knitting and often got stuck with my latest project. I always took the knitting problem to my mother who patiently sorted it, no matter how many knots she found. I look back and see myself at that time as a knotted ball of wool – my body, mind and spirit were all affected by grief; I was full of knots. I found it was definitely best to bring them out into the open and get them untangled and smoothed.

Rachel was now in her second year at her school, which was a five-minute drive away from home. After we'd been back from Bristol for a few weeks, she gradually settled back into school routine, but not without difficulty. Until then, she had never been particularly keen on playgroup or school and much preferred staying at home. I found it hard to tell what was really going on with her, whether this was linked with Russ's death or not. The headmistress was helpful; she knew Rachel well and recognized her innate strong-mindedness. Like many young children, she had a tendency to manipulate as she began to find her way in life, and I had to balance this against my instinctive knowledge that she wasn't always fully up to the demands of school. Grief is a tiring process, and Rachel was grieving. So I sometimes notified the school that I was keeping her home, and we would have a 'Daddy Time' when we talked about Russ, looked at pictures and videos and spoke about our feelings. I don't regret any of those times. In my desire to do the best for my children, I considered home schooling, moving Rachel to a closer school or even moving house, but finally decided to continue with the familiar routine. And apart from the first month or two when her concentration was affected, Rachel's school reports reflected stability, consistency and very good progress. As for Lucy, she went to a little nursery twice a week for a few hours, which seemed to be enough for her. I felt she also needed the reassurance of plenty of time with me, and the opportunity to explore her feelings and release her emotions. All this time I kept alive for her the memories of her daddy by talking about him, showing videos and photos and repeatedly highlighting her own memories of them together. But underneath the surface, my own grief was bubbling and moving. It was only when Lucy began one full day a week at nursery six months after Russ died that I could take time to deal with my own pain, to lie on the floor and wail out torrents of pent-up grief. Thank goodness we had a detached house! Sometimes I played Christian music, always aware of God's presence and comfort. This process could last minutes or even hours, and I didn't care which.

In the early weeks I felt as though we had a funnel through the roof of our sitting room connecting me directly with heaven. I would sit on the same rug I had knelt upon during those early mornings before Russ's diagnosis when I would reaffirm my commitment to follow God. One night while I was sleeping I had the sensation of being cocooned and awoke to the continuing sense of being completely enveloped. I knew God was holding me, and guessed he was healing me. The sensation lasted a few days, and the impact remains.

Over the following months we cried whenever we needed to, all together and apart. On one occasion Rachel said, 'I need to look after you, Mummy.'

I replied quickly, 'No, Rachel, you are *my* responsibility. It is me that will look after *you*.' I would not have her feeling responsible for me.

She would sometimes lie awake crying in bed until late, and I will never forget hearing those agonizing sobs as I held her while she poured out her grief. She often cried when I felt most tired and lacking in resources. In the beginning I didn't know how to handle this, or how I would ever bear seeing my own child in such pain. It was just too awful.

At bedtime on 5 January 2001 I sat in the girls' room watching them drift into sleep. I dipped into *The Secret of Happy Children* by Steve Biddulph[3] and my eyes fell on a passage which stressed the importance of allowing grieving children to cry and just to be there for them. This really helped me. It said that within the last ten years since it was written, it had been discovered that endorphins are released when we cry in this way. These emotional tears block pain receptors and produce a measure of healing anaesthesia through the worst of the anguish that loss can bring. This effect is closely related to the effects of morphine and can be as powerful. I later read some words from Mary Pytches, a counsellor and author. She wrote that scientists have reported discovering a marked difference between tears shed through emotion and those from the peeling of onions – the latter contain no chemicals from the endorphin family whatsoever.[4]

As soon as I had read Steve Biddulph's words, Rachel suddenly began to cry in the most agonizing way I have ever known. With the benefit of what I'd just read, I allowed her tears to flow and they lasted for a full twenty minutes. Her little body was absolutely wracked with grief. Then, as at previous times when she had cried, she stopped suddenly, and came out with an unrelated comment about something that had happened that day. That was such a lesson to me – that tears do eventually stop – and so I found the strength to hang on in there.

Support was always there for me, in the right ways and at the right times, and I believe God made sure of it. My family and friends were amazing. I received unexpected offers of assistance; many people wanted to help, as they'd done when Russ was ill. Although my brother lived in the States, he phoned me regularly when he got to work, and my sister, Jackie, frequently called, willing to listen to my feelings. They both wanted to help me with decisions. I had never found some decisions easy, and now they seemed harder than ever without Russ. This was probably the hardest daily battle I faced – knowing what to do for the best. Russ's family were grieving too and we kept in close contact, although I think we tried to protect each other from our pain. It became easier to speak together about Russ as time moved on.

Practical support was especially welcome. One friend turned up with two bags of food for me every few weeks. Initially she kept in contact every few days and sometimes helped me in the kitchen or with a bit of decorating. She continued to ring me regularly. Another friend brought me home-cooked meals, and a mum from school stood at the foot of my stairs with arms ready to take my laundry. My neighbour said he would clean my car weekly. All this help was so much appreciated because these wonderful people didn't leave me feeling beholden to them; they'd offered specific help, and all I needed to do was accept. With so much responsibility suddenly landing on my shoulders it was hard to work out what I needed, much less ask for it, and I accepted each offer gratefully. Another neighbour turned up with his fire extinguisher when the fat became dangerously overheated in my grill; a nearby friend came to rescue our cat from inside our roof-space, and to open Rachel's door when she'd mischievously removed her doorknob. Although it's amusing to recount these incidents now, at the time each caused me to panic and invariably, pray. My sister-in-law, Anne, often popped in on her way back from work. Russ's sister supported me, even though she was grieving herself. A semi-retired relative phoned every few weeks to see how I was, and came to play with Lucy so I could deal with paperwork. A few others regularly rang and took particular interest in the girls. Our friends Jackie and Jerry would meet us all for a fun outing, perhaps a long country walk with their dog, or a trip to the climbing wall. The first time I did each thing without Russ was always the hardest, but I needed to continue to take the girls out and about.

Another milestone was being able to stay on my own at night with the girls. I had felt very vulnerable at the beginning, and reassured myself by writing my neighbour's number on the bedroom phone. Around this time two schoolgirls went missing, and this heightened my anxiety now I was a single parent. With time, I've learnt to trust God more in this area.

I found it easiest to talk to people I knew well. Some openly admitted they didn't know what to say, and I always said, 'That's fine. You don't have to say anything, just listen!' It was far easier for me when friends listened rather than saying something unhelpful out of embarrassment. Often I found myself encouraging the person speaking to me, to put them at ease. Some bereaved people say how others crossed the road to avoid them. This wasn't my experience, and I found that mothers from school, people I barely knew, were often very understanding and related their experiences in a helpful way. Nevertheless, I found the daily chats at the school gate tiring, particularly early on.

As a newly bereaved widow some comments were hard for me to handle. Almost immediately someone said, 'Well, you have the children.' Of course I did, and I loved them deeply, but that was separate from losing my husband. Those comments made me feel guilty for not appreciating the children enough, and I wished people wouldn't make assumptions when they spoke to me. Russ and I had always tried to put God first in our relationship, and each other second. We were a unit, and that unit was now broken. In time I would, of course, see how having the girls helped me tremendously, but when Russ died they were 5 and 3. I needed immense resources to care for them, and they were too young to give any appreciation back to me. All I could see was that a vital part of our family was missing, and I felt I was floundering as a single parent. I knew I could care for them, but didn't know how to *manage* my new situation. Two weeks after Russ had died I had asked God for another daddy. Now, I asked him again – and again. It wasn't that I could replace him so easily, and Russ would have chuckled at this. It was because I honestly didn't know how to be a family without a father.

18

THE FIRST YEAR

Four months had passed since Russ's death, and the children were gradually adapting to their new way of life without him. Spring was in the air, and to Rachel it seemed a long time since Daddy had died. She commented, 'It happened before Christmas.' Four months was a long time in her short life.

At this time I wrote in my journal that she seemed settled at school although she wasn't happy for anyone else to drive her there, despite offers from other mothers. Lucy attended nursery twice a week but preferred being at home with me. To this day she remembers how thrilled she was on the day we arrived at nursery to find the door locked. We had to return home because we weren't able to make ourselves heard above the hullabaloo inside. Lucy was doing her fair share of grieving, saying every few days how she missed her daddy. When left alone with certain people she would tell them, 'My daddy has died.' At times it did seem that she started to cry when Rachel and I did, to feel part of things, but at other moments I would find her singing quietly to herself, 'I wish my daddy was here.' From time to time a loud outburst would erupt from the depths of her being, and I would hold her until the tears subsided.

Lucy missed her special friend from the playgroup in Bristol, a girl whose sister had been in hospital at the same time as Russ. Her mother and I had kept in touch, and one day we met up with our children on a visit to the hospital playgroup. We were warmly welcomed by the staff and I thanked them again for their skill and understanding, which played such a big part in my daughters' fond memories of Bristol.

Winston's Wish, the leading childhood bereavement charity in the UK, offers a wide range of practical support and bereavement guidance to children, their families and professionals. I had already contacted them when Russ had been rushed to hospital, and the people there soon became a part of our lives. They sent Sarah, a family support worker, to visit us in our home every few weeks. On Sarah's third visit she gave us three large 'memory boxes' with space on the front for a photo of Russ, and she suggested we fill them with special memorabilia of our lives together. The boxes came in different colours and designs. Rachel chose bright yellow, encircled with forget-me-nots, saying, 'I'm not going to forget my daddy.' Lucy decided on the underwater pattern, 'Because Daddy loved the sea, and I love him.'

I chose a functional brown box – because Russ had suited autumnal shades, and even his wedding outfit had been brown. I smiled, remembering how he would add a splash of panache with a zany tie to his suit.

Sarah's visits lasted about an hour and a half, during which she would encourage us to put our memories of Russ into words, so as to reinforce them. She showed us how to make a salt jar, made up of layers of different colours of salt, each representing a separate memory. The children would have the opportunity for individual time with her – which Rachel particularly welcomed; she often spoke about school. After a while the girls would disappear to their rooms, leaving Sarah to speak with me alone. I usually cried, focusing on my pain and grief, yet also expressing my hope in Christ. I would tell her, 'I do have a real sense of God's love and tremendous security because I feel he's looking after me.'

The girls and I attended a Winston's Wish family event – a performance at the beautifully ornate Victorian Everyman Theatre in Cheltenham. That was our first family event with them, and I found it very moving to be amongst 300 bereaved people, seated together in the stalls. There were goodie bags for the girls and even a box of chocolates for me as a parent. This touch of warmth meant such a lot. In the interval I noticed another mother working hard to contain her lively son. I introduced myself and found she had two children even younger than mine. By coincidence her husband, also called Russell, had died suddenly too. Gazing across the sea of faces, I considered how the majority of children were there because their father had died. Others had known mother, sibling or grandparent die.

Once I had overcome my apprehension of joining in for the first time, we came to really value the Winston's Wish events. As single parents, it was complicated to arrange to meet up with the mother I had met at the theatre, but we did manage a spring evening pub walk in the Cotswolds organized by the charity. On that occasion we talked non-stop about our husbands. Along the way we met up with others and had a pub supper outside. I particularly remember chatting to a widow on a nearby table and noticing that she didn't wear her wedding ring. It struck me that the day would come when I too would remove mine.

During April I renewed my acquaintance with Julie, the wife of a man called Robin who I'd been privileged to nurse before he died in the Sue Ryder hospice. Like Russ, Robin had become a Christian in adult life. We had so much in common, and gradually our friendship grew to the point where I felt able to phone her early in the morning when my pain on waking was too much to bear. As a dog owner, Julie could be counted on to be up and about on cold dark mornings. Often in tears, I would tell her how awful I felt, and how I still couldn't believe Russ had died.

I said, 'It feels like a massive black boulder is sitting bang in front of me, totally obscuring any view.'

It still comforts me to remember her soothing words, 'I know, Judy, I know. The pain will go, Judy; it *will* go.'

In 2 Corinthians 1:4, Paul speaks of comforting one another with the comfort that we ourselves have received, and Julie was a very real example of this in my life. I bought a CD around this time, called *Beautiful Tapestry* by Robert Critchley. I often played a track called 'What a faithful God,' which really helped me. Later I read that Robert wrote it after his newborn son, Gideon, had died. Other tracks spoke to me of the love and comfort of God. I read that this music reminded Robert of when he'd experienced God's comforting presence as a boy, on the day his father died. There were several CDs which helped me and I played one which spoke clearly of heaven over and over again.

During that first spring I found solace in art, music and nature. One memorable morning I was enchanted to see how expanses of forget-me-nots had suddenly blossomed in both our front and back gardens. A clump or two had sprung up the previous year but nothing to compare with this picture which would continue to surprise and delight us for many years to come.

Country walks helped enormously, although I had to plan my route carefully as foot and mouth infection had broken out in England, and many fields were out of bounds. I gained real pleasure from a pot of bulbs I'd been given in the autumn and which were now blooming. I hadn't been able to bring myself to plant up any pots – that was Russ's forte and I wasn't ready to take over that role. Planting bulbs would have involved planning ahead. I wasn't ready to move forward myself, although I kept in step with the children's progress.

That spring I heard Bishop David Pytches, former vicar of St Andrew's, Chorleywood (and husband of Mary), speak at a service. I knew he had seen the Lord bring healing to many people over the years. Afterwards I spoke to him about my grief and he gave me some helpful advice: 'You just have to go through it, my dear.' He was saying that my grief would not disappear instantly and, although it was hard to hear, I knew he was right.

I continued to wonder if God had someone in mind to be a father to the girls and a husband to me. On the odd social occasion I attended I still felt very much *Russ's wife* and the whole idea of someone else seemed too strange, yet I admit that if my path had led me to an early second marriage, one that I felt was right for me and the girls, I would have gladly taken it.

I honestly did sense the presence of God every day, and felt him taking care of us. Even in those early months I sometimes felt his joy bubbling up in me, and other people seemed to catch it. That happened on the day my neighbour called for coffee. He and his wife were moving house, but that cold but sunny morning I caught sight of him transferring the last few items from his garage to his car, and called out, 'Would you like a coffee?'

'I'll be right over,' he replied.

I was a little surprised as I'd intended to take the coffee out to him. To be honest, I was also nervous; ours was the kind of relationship that operated from the safety of my kitchen window. In the morning when I opened my kitchen blind, I'd wave to him and his wife and we would occasionally meet outside, exchanging pleasantries.

Now he came into my kitchen, and I found myself speaking to him about Russ's life and death. He listened intently, and started asking questions about Jesus. Suddenly, we both became aware of being bathed in the most amazing sense of the presence of God.

I quietly whispered, 'God's here.'

He replied, 'I know. That's why I came.'

Before long, he was praying, and asking for forgiveness for his sins. I prayed for him to be filled with the Holy Spirit and told him that he too would be in heaven one day as he continued to follow Christ. We sat motionless for what seemed like an age, with God's presence filling that room. As he left, I knelt down and gave thanks to God. Russ's death had played a part in this man coming to know Christ; already our situation was producing fruit for God's glory.

These are some journal entries from that spring of 2001:

18 February
Today was hard. Saw a red Vauxhall Cavalier like our old one and could almost see Russ reversing into drive. I miss him, my Boaz protector, not because I desperately need someone to love me. I don't (I guess I have my girls). I miss him because I love him. But I too will be in heaven one day. I know God will look after me and the girls here in the meantime.

19 February
Russ's family arranged a social get-together and everyone was very kind, but I desperately wanted to see Russ

appear at the door. On our return home, friends called. Told them how I felt. 'Trust God,' they urged. That helped.

20 February
Only now am I really questioning why.

25 March
Feel like I'm on a tightrope. Crazy day: told off dentist, panic as income being adjusted, washing machine stopped, power cut – house in darkness, saw Bible on table and a split second thought surfaced, 'How do I know it is true?' It went as quick as it came, as I do know.

28 March
Five months now. Today the pain is awful. Tears just streaming. Really hit rock bottom. Someone called it 'despair'. It needed to come out. Sooo hard – as if I was using all my strength to scratch bare fingernails on old rusty metal . . . again and again – paint all gone and only the base raw metal left. Didn't feel angry but just knew I was hitting rock bottom. Felt an enormous pain in my stomach and asked Val to pray with me. As she did, the word 'hope' was etched on my mind and she prayed about this. Sense of pain as the next layer comes to the surface . . . and tears gush.

30 March
Tears and pain of last two days are gone. Feel so much better. Today so calm and together. Incredible! Sense of Russ's love close to me – more so than if he was out at work. I guess because Jesus is here and he is with Jesus. Looked up Peter Marshall's words about presence of loved ones with the Lord, 'For if they are with thee, and thou art with us, how can they be very far away?'[5] (Catherine Marshall's

first husband, Peter, was a young Scottish immigrant who became chaplain of the United States Senate in the late 1940s. Her book about his life, *A Man Called Peter*, was full of inspiring passages which I lapped up at this time.)

24 April
First wedding anniversary since Russ's death. At home with Fiona, on leave from Zimbabwe – ideal – she was always so fond of Russ. Prayed and read from the Bible together. Fiona had a picture of God mending my heart – painstakingly sewing it together, stitch by stitch – would take time but pain would go. Great sense of peace.

25 April
I understood more about covenant love today, for just as I am committed to you, Lord, you are also committed to me. I pray I can use what I've learnt to proclaim you, Lord. I know I am loved and that you are my heavenly Father; I have no doubt that if I die today, I will be with you in heaven because I trust in Christ. I do know you will bring good and glory to your name through all this.

29 April
Watched video with girls – *The Tanglewoods' Secret* from Patricia St John's book – story of a little boy dying but living on in heaven. Struck by shepherd's words – 'If you had a sheep and it was on rough pasture, wouldn't you take it to the good and safe pasture?'[6] Sense this happened to my Russ, remembering a friend's prayer the night before he died . . . he 'saw' stairs rising upwards and strongly sensed Russ would die, but was being delivered.

10 June
Felt God prompting me to read the *The Helper*, by Catherine Marshall – about the comforting role of the

Holy Spirit. Timely, as Lucy needed comforting after bursting into tears when she'd bumped her knee and caught sight of a photo of Daddy. A special time – I prayed for us to receive more of the Holy Spirit.

12 June
Another significant dream. The girls and I walked down a corridor and Russ was at the end, wearing a large brown check shirt and trousers. As Rachel approached him, I was aware of deep love between them. Russ had tears in his eyes and then Lucy ran up to him; it was wonderful.

Awoke feeling beautifully rested and as if I am floating on air, a wonderfully warm godly feeling. Remembered Russ treasuring his special time with each of the girls the Monday night before he died.

26 June
When Russ died I wanted to be in heaven. Then I wanted life as it was before his illness. Now I want to live my life for Christ and walk with him more closely.

Rachel and I had a good chat about Russ. She had prayed about some things at school and told me, 'When you pray, Mummy, you're really praying!'

15 July
I feel very, very raw, like a slab of meat. Woke early and flung myself into the silence and emptiness. So many things to do . . . who to call . . . my eyes hurt . . . too many things on my mind. Tears flow. In the reaching out of myself I find God, who warms my soul, and I am helped. I feel like Shadrach and his friends in the fiery furnace . . . I am in it, yet not being burned. I am facing the emptiness and in it I find my God. I'm thinking of Betsie, on that stretcher, before she died 'There is no pit so deep that God is not deeper still.'[7]

◆   ◆   ◆

During this time I often went to bed soon after the girls, and found it comforting to read myself to sleep with inspirational books by Christian widows, including several by Catherine Marshall. After ten years of widowhood, she took the brave step of marrying a man with three young children. Her second husband, Len LeSourd, later wrote in the book, *Light in My Darkest Night:*[8] 'It was not a sense of her own adequacy that impelled her – on the contrary, she was all too aware of her shortcomings as a wife and mother. It was the certainty that "God was adequate."' This encouraged me that God would be adequate in my situation.

Len also quotes Catherine speaking of her relationship with Christ during a family tragedy: 'I need you and your presence in my life more than I need understanding.' This phrase was such a help to me after I woke early one morning wrestling yet again with the thought, 'Should Russ have been discharged from Bristol?' Yes, I needed Christ more than understanding! I identified with Catherine who decided to trust God to give her an answer to all her 'why's' – but only if and when he chose.

Time meandered on. That first summer I crammed in fun activities for the girls, and we travelled far and wide enjoying some very special times – including a trip to the States to see my brother. Returning home was difficult, but I did know God loved me and that he was near.

I still cried often, but less frequently in front of the girls, who would say, 'Oh no, not more tears!' Stopping was sometimes hard, but I tried to quell my tears now in front of them. Rachel still cried on occasions when she was tucked up in bed and sometimes it lasted a while.

The dreaded first anniversary of Russ's death came around and Fiona, who was still in England, came with me to a Christian day conference in Dudley. It was led by John and Carol Arnott. Afterwards I wrote in my journal, 'Something significant has happened. Carol spoke of her experience of suddenly being left alone to raise two young children. She prayed with me afterwards: I had a profound realization that the Lord was being Father to the girls and husband to me.'

When I got home from this conference, I was surprised to find a slip from the library on my doormat; the book I'd ordered had arrived. It was *To Live Again* by Catherine Marshall.[9] I was struck by the appropriateness of the title – a year had now passed, and I truly wanted to live again.

The following day, Fiona and I walked up Cleeve Hill to scatter Russ's ashes around the spot on our 'holy hill' where he had made his commitment all those years before. It was the same spot where he had asked me to be his wife that summer's evening nine and a half years earlier. From our vantage point I could see the mushroom farm where he'd worked, as well as our home.

Fiona read a psalm and I scattered the ashes, and there were more than I'd expected. A bird sang overhead in the nearby tree as we planted some crocus bulbs underneath in the mossy ground. The moment felt so very precious.

On the way home I collected the book from the library. On the cover was a picture of a tree and immediately I thought of our tree on the hill, where I'd just scattered Russ's ashes. Reading the book later that evening, I was drawn to some words Catherine had written soon after her husband had died. She was caring for their son, 6-year-old Peter John. 'But deeper than fear, was the sure knowledge that from the moment of

Peter's death, God had taken over Peter John and me in a new way.' This sentence was an affirmation to me of the impression God had made on my own heart the day before. It was comforting to identify with another person who had been through the same grieving process as me.

The same sense of comfort came from many individuals and support groups. Although each individual story of loss is unique, I've since found that many other people have navigated a similar route to mine. I'm travelling along a path that's well-trodden by those who have gone before me; some will walk with me and others will follow after. We are not alone on our journey.

As I sank into bed that night I turned out the light and breathed out slowly and deeply. I had made it through the first year.

19

SHADOWLANDS

Over the next six months my emotions were on a bit of a roller coaster. The fourteenth and fifteenth months since Russ had died seemed easier to bear, and I felt well on the way to coming to terms with his death. Then February dawned, and I was shocked to find that the pain was as bad as at the start, though for less prolonged periods. One crisp morning a kind friend of my parents phoned to see how I was. She had known loss herself and made a point of phoning me now and then. She'd previously warned me, 'Of course, you may be different, Judy, but I found the second year was worse as that's when reality sets in.' I hadn't liked hearing that, but now her words helped me to see my experience as normal.

My next-door neighbours had moved away, leaving me with a sense that some things were changing; life was already different from when the children were tiny. Although I was sad to leave familiar things behind, experiencing fresh circumstances really helped me to move on.

My church members were very caring, and helped me tremendously. They were very prayerful and practical, helping me with babysitting and cat-sitting. Some of them had suffered a different kind of significant loss in their lives – a marriage breakdown. The close of the morning service would find me seeking those individuals whose shoulder I could cry on, people with whom I could be real, knowing that in some ways they understood. I would often find myself staring at the piano, as I pictured Russ standing there playing the cornet or preaching at the front. Only now he wasn't there. We had worshipped together in that church for twelve years and I still couldn't adjust to life apart from him.

On some Sunday evenings I managed to have a short break to attend nearby Trinity Church, where I would take the opportunity to have prayer for healing at the end of the service. Here I felt free from responsibility as I knew the girls were being cared for at home. Although I knew God was gently healing me day by day, these times of special prayer and worship were a great encouragement. At my own church, I had the responsibility of the girls, a heightened sense of others' needs, and constant memories of Russ. Also, as our church membership was relatively small at that time, Russ's absence seemed very pronounced.

During this period Lucy went through a phase of shedding deep, painful tears, and Rachel often crept in to me at night, crying. After their grief had found its expression, it would ebb away, and they seemed to move on quickly. They had begun to call God their 'Heavenly Daddy' and sometimes referred to Russ as 'Daddy Two'. I found myself introducing the possibility of another future father as Daddy Three, which worked for a while until I heard Lucy say, 'But I want This Daddy.' I too wanted *This* Daddy.

The biggest comfort of all for us was the certainty that Russ was alive with Christ and sharing in Christ's victory over death. Although Russ had been a believer for a number of years, in my work I had known people choose to turn to Christ in the last hours of their lives, even when they had to use means of communication other than words. I had been privileged to glimpse a little of how God spoke to people in those moments, and to be aware that we can never know what takes place between a person and God in the last seconds of someone's life.

The girls drew many pictures of heaven at this time. Rachel sketched one of Russ passing from death to life, and said to me, 'Mummy, I think Daddy closed his eyes here and opened them in heaven.'

The children valued their memory boxes from Winston's Wish and often rummaged through them. We spoke about Russ frequently and in their 'Daddy Times' new memories still surfaced. One day Rachel told me a school friend had asked her, 'How does it feel to have no daddy?' A lump formed in my throat. It didn't seem fair that she should have to handle that. Although I knew it was said with childhood curiosity, it was painful to hear. I asked Rachel how it had made her feel, and she intimated that she hadn't dwelt on it, and it was fine. Later, as I looked back, I realized that sometimes I was hurt on the girls' behalf when they were actually OK. They seemed able to get on with daily life and yet still value the times we remembered Russ. We were grieving together, but the way the children experienced and dealt with it was different to mine.

From time to time Lucy and Rachel had special dreams of Russ. Sometimes we asked God for a dream about Daddy, and the dream that came could be a very real encouragement. Rachel had a lovely dream in which he had died and yet suddenly re-appeared, very much alive, wearing his green pyjamas 'with gold things on'. 'When we got home together, he swung me and Lucy on a rope.'

e.g. Michelle Oliver, at 42, 'I'm going to dance again — She'd denied God's existence!

I asked, 'How do you feel about the dream?'

'Good, happy. He was very, very alive.'

One of Lucy's dreams took place when she was just over 5 years old. She eagerly related the details to me the following morning and I recorded them word for word:

> I was in a swimming pool but couldn't swim so I had blue things and arm bands. Rachel and Mummy and Daddy swam under the sea. Sometimes I sank, but Daddy caught my feet. Jesus came and the people who were swimming stood in a line to shake his hand. I was shy. Jesus put out his hand, and Daddy took my hand and put my hand in Jesus' and shook it for me. I put something into Daddy's hand as I didn't want him to shake my hand for me. I bent down, looking over his shoulder, and I shook Jesus' hand; Jesus grew bigger. He was so kind, as when he grew bigger I grew bigger too. Jesus pretended I was a giant, but I was really, really tiny. Jesus had two sparkles in his hands for Rachel and me. They were in our favourite colours, pink and yellow. Then all the rest went home and that was the end and I waked up.

In her Winston's Wish book, Rachel recorded special memories of what Daddy liked doing. There was also a section on expressing anger. She did get angry and frustrated at times, and this was usually directed at me when I challenged her. I found it particularly hard when she once said, 'I wish you'd died instead of Daddy.' The stab of hurt caused by her immature outburst was over in a second, eclipsed by that continual gnawing pain in the depth of my being of losing Russ.

The children's after-school activities had begun to wane. Instead, they wanted freedom, time to play with friends, and lots of cuddles. In my journal I wrote, 'They

both seem very happy. I have continued with a computer course, taking assignments and some speaking
opportunities as they come up.'

As February came to an end, I managed to pass an
evening without tears, and there was a spring in my step
as I sensed God was cementing truths within me about
the times to come. I made frequent journal entries, feeling that one day soon I would begin to write about
Russ's story and all that we had experienced. I always
knew the story would be underpinned by my awareness
of eternity and the deep joy that's been present throughout my grief, albeit interwoven with pain.

I watched the video of *Shadowlands* – the film about
C.S. Lewis losing his wife, Joy – for perhaps the tenth
time. It showed how C.S. Lewis had blocked out the
pain of his mother's death, and in doing so, had blocked
off part of himself, making it hard to express emotion
and be vulnerable later in life. He asks, 'Why love if losing hurts so much?' In response to his wife's death, he
chose a different path, one of facing the pain. His wife's
honesty had enabled him to do this, and as the film ends
he declares, 'The boy chose safety, the man chooses suffering: the pain now is part of the happiness then.'[10]

This expression of C.S. Lewis' grief was invaluable to
me. Although I didn't think I was feeling angry with
God, I needed to express the rawness of my emotions,
and the portrayal of Lewis's honesty helped me to do
this. In the film, a vicar and colleague, Harry, finds it
unsettling to witness Lewis's deep emotion and, very
shortly after Joy's death, declares, 'Life must go on.'

C.S. Lewis replies, 'I don't know that it must, Harry,
but it certainly does.' Harry's bland words about how
God cares, and that we see so little here, are delivered in
such a condescending way that C.S. Lewis flies at him,
going further and saying, 'No, we are the rats in the

cosmic laboratory . . . it's a bloody awful mess and that's all there is to it!'

Harry shakes his head, feeling C.S. Lewis has gone too far, whereas, in fact, it is Harry who has used the provoking words. That scene helped me so much. Russ had died and I didn't want platitudes, just truth. It was a terrible, terrible mess – even when I felt hope within it.

Journal entries at this time include:

I didn't read these as I don't want to feel guilty.

24 January 2002

I'm angry at you for leaving me. Why did you do it? Did you think it was some kind of joke? It's so hard here. Why isn't their daddy here to help us with the computer, DIY and more? He's in a better place. How can I stay here? I want to go. I miss him so much. I can't believe he's gone.

God seems to be saying that he hears my cry, that he is my father and he loves me. I don't understand now, but I will later. I need to hold his hand and he will lead me to greener pastures. I need to trust him and he will do it. Russ is with him. I need not wish him back. I think God is saying there was a 'rightness' in his going – for the next chapter to unfold.

21 February 2002

Feel in transition, midway between caterpillar and butterfly, wings all crumpled. Fine in Tesco's till Rachel's teacher asked how I really was. Found note Russ had written to me in 'Bethany' (our first home) about God being a shield. Spring in step later. Glad lounge carpet needs replacing, as need to change something, maybe even move. Felt real hole in my heart on Monday. Felt lot of pain and debris gone and wound clean, open for healing. Girls have no problems at school; it's heaven! Awoke yesterday morning and couldn't believe Russ had died. Dwelling on medical details yet again. Lasted two hours tonight without tears.

8 March 2002
Feeling better this last week. Coping with comments like, 'Of course, you never really get over it,' or, 'A friend is only just improving after four years.' Cried as I drove past Castle Ashby, remembering our wedding night and our gifts to each other – the leather case for him and the leather Bible for me. Went on to dwell on the following morning, our first as man and wife, when he made a time and place for us to honour God together in Bible reading and prayer. Metaphorically grabbed those painful memories and hurled them at God to deal with. After ten minutes felt better!

15 March 2002
Girls and I having lovely times together. We often remember Russ without the need to shed tears. If I cry at home, Rachel brings me Misty, our cat, for comfort. Wept during prayer at church – how would I cope with the future? Soon felt wonderfully comforted. Feeling like a mole, pushing my nose up for air and light and longing to move on from all this.

25 April 2002
Missionary friends have visited – such an encouragement. They sense God preparing me for new paths ahead. Realize living in past might impede the new life which he has planned.

31 May 2002
Many practical concerns. Sad time as Mum has been in hospital – lots of driving to and fro. Now improving and girls generally fine. Rachel cried tonight watching

Joseph being reunited with his dad in the musical – part of her grief pattern. For me it is *Shadowlands* and a few other films which bring identification. So grateful for the comfort they bring.

Feel delighted, yet also, selfishly, slightly bereft; the girl I met at Winston's Wish has met someone new. Seems quick to me because of where I am in my grief. Julie's going to marry Peter. So happy for her – it will be different for me. Think it's because she's been so with me in the grief and now she won't be a widow any more.

In time our circumstances too will change. For now I want to hold on to Russ. I still see him in my mind as he returns home at the end of the day. I need to look intently at his photos and long to talk with him, to finish it all off somehow. I pour my heart out to Christ, still hardly believing it has happened. I ask God why, and my gaze moves to the windows where I see crosses in the wooden design.

Began preface for book today. Felt encouraged as I prayed about it. Believe God is re-establishing my individual identity. Isaiah 42:9 from the Bible sticks in my mind, 'the former things have taken place, and new things I declare'.

20

MOVING FORWARD

As 2002 progressed, Rachel and Lucy settled more happily into school. I managed to make ends meet, helped
by timely bags of girls' second-hand clothes, unexpected
gifts and holiday treats. Before Russ died we had lived
on a tight budget, so I was used to managing. I decorated a room and did my best to maintain the home and
finances. Although I'd lived alone in a small house for
two and a half years before marrying Russ, I now had a
family to consider, and it was very much a learning time.

It didn't seem practical or right at that point to take a
return to nursing course, and I managed to get by with
money from insurance policies, widow's allowance and
child tax credit. I even made savings from tax returns
and succeeded in converting my remaining endowment
mortgage to repayment. I continued with my computer
course, writing this book and going to writing work-
shops. Whenever there was an opportunity to speak at
church, I accepted, and enjoyed using the theological
training which I felt privileged to have received. It felt
right to let my nursing skills lie fallow at that time.
Because I had cared for Russ so intimately, I wasn't

ready to return to that career so soon. But as every
month passed I enjoyed speaking of my faith in Christ
more and more.

hm? (handwritten note in left margin)

I continued to share my pain with those who understood, although with Russ's family I still held back in
case I made them more upset. In hindsight I think frank-
ness is always better, and as time went on, we did speak
of Russ more openly. Two friends who work for
Listening Post set aside some evenings to be available to
me.

Once, when I was feeling guilty that I should have
contacted the doctor earlier or prevented Russ's discharge from Bristol, I asked friends to pray with me. As
they prayed, I remembered these words from the New
Testament, 'there is now no condemnation for those who
are in Christ Jesus' (Rom. 8:1) and I felt reassured and
peaceful. Two days later I tuned into the morning radio
service to hear, once again, 'There is now no condemnation for those who are in Christ Jesus.'

That same morning as I attended church, I sensed
God speaking to me through the story of Joseph. His
brothers had left him in a pit; Joseph later told them not
to fear, for although they had done wrong to their brother, God had used Joseph's trial for good, and he had
sent him ahead to save people's lives. Somehow, that
spoke into my situation with an assurance that I sensed
came from God. I could blame others or myself, but God
had a plan to use my situation for good. HE ALWAYS HAS

One evening, as I was driving the girls back from a
swimming lesson, a car suddenly appeared very close to
us, seemingly out of nowhere, and we narrowly avoided
a collision. That incident made me appreciate what I *did*
have. I asked myself, rather sharply, 'Judy – are you
going to waste the next twenty years wallowing over
anything you could have done to prevent Russ dying?

Are you going to allow that to affect your peace as you look after the girls?'

Even though I knew the major decisions had been in the hands of the doctors, I made a promise to myself to try to stop this unhealthy focus on Russ – the questions and unwarranted guilt – and instead to move forward and concentrate on my daughters and our future.

As summer progressed, I realized I was emerging from three months of real pain. I remember sitting in a friend's garden, admiring the abundance of richly green leaves on the trees as I gazed over a lane where Russ and I used to drive. I was reminded of Amy Carmichael who wrote that it is actually in the winter time that you see through the branches to what is beyond. I felt as if I'd gone into the beyond with Russ, and was now returning to tell the story. I thought, 'One day this beyond will be reality. Now I only have the imprint of the depth and richness of that experience. To discover what is beyond it takes winter and walking the path of need.' At the same time, my former vicar spoke these wise words to me: 'First, God is sovereign. Second, Russ does not need you now. Third, your priority from God is to the girls.'

During September 2002 I met with the chaplain at Cheltenham hospital, where Russ had died. I told him about my grief and my constant need to review the details of Russ's death over and over in my mind. He shared a helpful illustration with me: 'Think about a video which is gradually wearing out because it's been played and replayed. The same process applies to our grief, Judy.'

While I was leafing through some of my brother's books, I came across *Emotional Intelligence* by Daniel Goleman, where the following passage now made a lot of sense

Patients need to mourn the loss the trauma brought . . . The mourning that ensues while retelling such painful events serves a crucial purpose; it marks the ability to let go of the trauma itself to some degree. It means that instead of being perpetually captured by this moment in the past, patients can start to look ahead, even to hope, and to rebuild a new life free of the trauma's grip. It is as if the constant recycling and reliving of the trauma's terror by the emotional circuitry were a spell that could finally be lifted. Every siren need not bring a flood of fear . . . there are specific signs that the trauma has largely been overcome . . . being able to bear the feelings associated with memories . . . no longer having trauma memories erupt at uncontrollable moments, but rather being able to revisit them voluntarily . . . rebuilding a new life, with strong, trusting relationships and a belief system that finds meaning even in a world where such injustice can happen. All of these together are markers of success in reeducating the emotional brain.[11]

While I was sharing how I was still coming to terms with Russ's death, a kindly person would sometimes say, 'Maybe you never will.' I really hated that comment, feeling it would hang like a sentence over my head for the rest of this earthly life. It made me feel, 'I might as well just die now,' for the pain seemed unending. I did appreciate that those who said it meant to help, and later realized that although the imprint of Russ's death would never leave me fully, I would recover and the pain would indeed go.

That autumn brought a wonderful weekend away with Winston's Wish. This remarkable charity provided a safe and adventurous time away for children who had lost a close relative. The girls stayed with about thirty other children, plus trained workers and volunteers, and had a programme of different activities to help them remember and express feelings about their daddy, the highlights being the campfire and scaling a wall. Twenty parents and I also enjoyed the weekend away, staying nearby in a setting also organized by Winston's Wish. We enjoyed a meal and time to ourselves, and for me it was the first night away from the children since Russ had died. We had a specially prepared programme in which we shared our stories, learning from each other and the Winston's Wish staff. The girls and I found ourselves in a similar situation to many others there, and that proved invaluable. It was a significant weekend for all of us, and I felt on the threshold of going forward. On the day we left I chose to wear a crisp lilac jumper, which reflected my new sense of hopefulness.

After going to camp, the children strongly associated themselves with Winston's Wish, and over the years we've attended several of their day trips. The Christmas Pantomime and Remembrance Time were particularly special, and Rachel made a star for Lucy and herself on the Winston's Wish website in memory of Russ.

When we came home from the weekend, Rachel and Lucy and I decided to make our familiar walk on Cleeve Hill to the special tree that had become 'Daddy's tree'. This time we took a few more crocus bulbs with us.

'They will flower in the spring,' I told the girls, 'and when we see them we'll remember Daddy.'

Rachel said, 'Do you remember when we came up here after Daddy died and played *Lion King* around the tree?'

'Yes, that would have made him laugh,' I said, remembering how painful yet moving it had been for me to sit there while they play-acted so soon after Russ had died. But however painful, during the last two years of grieving I had returned over and over to that tree on the hill. At that spot there were so many memories and connections with Russ: his proposal on that warm summer evening, his cry to God when he came off heroin, our last walk together only a week before his transplant. It hurt almost too much to be there, but I had to do it.

As 2002 came to a close, I wrote in my journal how my pain was ebbing and flowing more speedily. There were now occasions when I felt actual joy in what I was doing, such as when I was running with the girls, as well as the deep spiritual joy of worshipping God, even though I still missed Russ dearly. Often I used his turn of phrase when speaking with the girls, such as when he would tell them something and add the phrase, 'Did you know?' Some days I still expected him to walk through the front door for tea. Each time I wondered how long I had to endure this vain hope.

Alongside navigating our course of grief, I knew I had a special job, to look after my girls, and I was concerned to help them grow up with a living and vibrant faith. One day at church the preacher read a passage from the book of Genesis, and I was struck by Joseph's words to his brothers 'I will take care of you and your children' (Gen. 50:21, GNB). I'd been distracted by Lucy, and it seemed as if a loudspeaker had suddenly directed these words at me. I knew God was reassuring me about the girls' spiritual care and, like these words which were said by Joseph about his brothers' children, God wanted to tell me that he would look after me and my girls. Later on in the same service, some precious words were quoted from Colossians, about the peace of Christ guiding the people of God in decisions (see Col. 3:15, GNB). This confirmed my expectation that God would indeed guide me.

One morning I decided to take Lucy with me to a single parents' support day in Cardiff, with the theme The

Single Parent Journey. It was being led by the excellent organization Care for the Family, whose newsletters I'd been receiving for some time. This charity is committed to strengthening family life and helping those who face family difficulties. It has been supporting and encouraging families in the UK since 1988 through family-building events – attended by over three hundred thousand people – and through special initiatives for stepfamilies, single parents, bereaved parents and those parenting children with special needs.

When the day arrived, it was hard dropping Rachel off for her Brownie trip and driving eighty miles away from her with Lucy. Alongside my grief was the 'letting go' which all parents face as their children grow. This was the first trip away from me that Rachel had made, and the wrench was heightened by the fact that I was the sole parent. There was no father figure physically present to pick up the pieces if I got delayed, or who would carry the joint emotional responsibility. I was also aware that by attending the day, I was openly acknowledging the truth that I was a single parent. To embrace widowhood was one thing, but to face the reality of bringing up two children without a father was another. I was now taking the step of identifying with other single parents, each with a different story to tell, but linked to me and my own situation. Although my involvement in nursing and church had given me insight into the different ways families live, meeting some of these people had a profound effect on me. One woman had three children, one of whom needed special schooling; some women were divorced and had to deal with challenges from separation. Although the girls and I had endured the shock of having our established order wrenched away, the three of us had enjoyed a very loving home life with Russ, and we were very grateful for that.

At the support day Lucy was very well catered for, with children's activities in an adjacent room to the adult meeting. Christine Tufnell was head of Care for the Family's work with single parent families, and spoke of the change in circumstance that divorce or widowhood entails. Suddenly life has altered; it has been heading in one direction and has taken an abrupt turn that none of us had envisaged. I felt privileged to have been amongst the gathering, and returned home wiser and more realistic about my situation.

Autumn 2002 went out with a flurry of tears, coupled with a real sense of hope. One day, I was slowly sipping my coffee in the store where Russ had shopped so often. Suddenly I felt tears pricking my eyes and beginning to run down my cheeks. It was as if a dam of grief had burst its banks, its waters flowing in a powerful but silent rush. This time didn't feel like normal crying, and there was no sobbing, but I quietly stole my way out of the store. But later that same day I felt hope as I read some words by Amy Carmichael, stressing how special opportunities within a situation should never be wasted. I sensed the need to wait, and see what God would do through all of this.

21

STEPS TO RECOVERY

Spring 2003 arrived, and whenever I woke early to the sound of the dawn chorus, I invariably found myself crying.

If I spoke at one of the church services, I always took Russ's Bible with me. It was reassuring to have it beside me, in the same way that I was comforted by having his favourite jumper over my chair and wearing it from time to time. Russ's old shirts no longer featured as part of my wardrobe as they had at first. A friend from school began offering me first pickings from her bag of nearly new, quality clothes. This helped me financially and psychologically – it felt timely and liberating to put on a new and feminine outfit.

The girls were doing really well, and now talking naturally about Russ without even crying. Sometimes we impersonated him, taking turns to stand behind each other in the kitchen and tickle the top of one another's heads, the culprit quickly moving to pretend it wasn't them. Even little Lucy remembered him playing this game. At other times we played Lions, roaring and rolling around as he used to do with us. We all found it therapeutic to immerse ourselves in his quirky humour, re-enacting scenes from the past.

By May I felt a growing need for Russ's permission to let go and move on with my life. I asked the people who knew him best what they thought about this. His brother said, 'Of course you should move on.' Eira's letter expressed the same sentiment. Russ's mother and stepfather individually voiced their desire for us to move forward and look to the future. They even spoke of their hope of my finding another husband, and the children another father. I felt very touched by their generosity of spirit. I also began to see and understand that if Russ had lived, we would be moving forward rather than dwelling on the past. It was at this time I began to think, 'Living in the past is never healthy, whatever our circumstances.'

Eventually I knew I was ready to approach the consultant responsible for Russ in Cheltenham hospital. Some medical questions were still unanswered and I needed to know what had really happened, in order to lay things to rest in my mind. At last I felt able to handle the truth, and desperately wanted to hear it. This was serious. I didn't want platitudes; it felt vital for my ultimate recovery. I needed to get the circumstances of Russ's death clearer in my mind in order to be able to accept it fully. Some people I knew who'd been bereaved had said they would prefer to leave aspects of the medical care alone. But I needed to push my questions to the absolute limit, and that's what I did.

I vividly recall finding the consultant's return message on my answer phone: 'I understand you wish to talk to me about your husband's condition in the last days of his life. *Happy* to do so.'

This message was such a comfort to me that I saved it, and replayed it repeatedly over the following week. I think it was his openness which meant so much to me, and his willingness to meet with me brought a measure of healing before we even met. I made an appointment and asked Gail to come with me again, and bring the notes she'd taken of my conversation with the Bristol consultant soon after Russ's death.

At the hospital, we were led into a small room very similar to the one Russ and I had sat in the day after his diagnosis. My mind travelled back to the evening before that day, when our life changed in an instant after our family swim, with the doctor phoning to say he needed to visit.

The door of our room opened and the consultant greeted me warmly, armed with a great wad of Russ's hospital notes. My eyes fell on a red stamp on the cover of the file, marked 'Deceased'. My heart missed a beat. That word referred to Russ! I needed to see that word, for – however odd it sounds – until that moment I still hadn't fully taken in that he had died. This sudden shock actually helped me by reinforcing the reality. My husband was *deceased*.

The consultant answered my numerous medical questions clearly and very kindly. Nothing, it seemed, was hidden. He remembered Russ well, even though it was now over two and a half years since his death. We spent about an hour and a half together, going through the file, and I asked him many questions. My first was, 'Why did he pass out at home?'

'Russ's blood pressure was very low. The infection already had a very big hold.'

I asked him why it seemed to take so long to give him antibiotics, and I understood him to say that as Russ was in shock it took time to open the blood vessels. I learnt what I'd been told before, that the antibiotics and higher dose of steroids Russ was taking would have masked much of the infection. The consultant went into the medical details, giving me illuminating information about the inflammatory response to dead bacterial cells. This may have explained why Russ's legs became swollen so suddenly in Bristol. As we spoke, I was aware that for Russ there had only been a 50 per cent chance of survival after the transplant. And there would always have been further risk of illness.

The consultant concluded, 'All was done as it should be, Mrs Hopkins,' and these words were a real reassurance to me.

My final question was, 'Did he peacefully slip away?'

'Yes, most definitely, he did.'

As we got up and walked towards the door I gazed at the notes under his arm, and decided to risk a rebuff. I asked, rather sheepishly, 'Could I keep the notes a little longer?'

'Of course,' the consultant replied. 'Just drop them in at the office when you leave.' It was so easy.

I read all the notes in the file, particularly appreciating kind words written by the anaesthetist, which implied respect and admiration for Russ. When I handed the file back, I knew the consultant had finally sealed the door for me on the details of the last hours of Russ's earthly life. Only one question remained in my mind and I asked Gail, 'Could I have delayed Russ's trip home from Bristol?'

'Let's have a walk down to the hospital chapel,' she replied.

Once inside, we sat down, our eyes drawn to a large modern painting hanging on the wall in front of us. I was immediately struck by the drips of paint which had been allowed to fall on the canvass.

Gail asked, 'How do you feel about this painting – what do you think it's trying to convey?'

'Mostly I just want to mop up the paint drips.' As soon as I spoke the words, I saw a powerful correlation with my attitude to Russ's death. I said into space, 'I want to tie up all the loose ends, but I can't. I can't.'

My mind went back to my second visit to Bristol after Russ's death, when the consultant had told me, 'People die here too, Judy.' He had meant that if Russ had remained there, he might well still have died.

I stared ahead blankly. I couldn't pretend it was easy, but as a Christian I was able to reconcile Russ's death with a loving God – knowing that with him suffering is never the final outcome. Christ died, yet his resurrection brings life and restoration. I knew God could have healed Russ physically, as nothing is impossible for him, but he had allowed him to die. I stared at the painting and realized I wouldn't know the reasons why – not here, not yet.

Gail and I talked about what I was feeling, and just before we left the chapel I imagined a box containing all my unanswered questions, placing it on the chair, and deliberately choosing to walk away from it. She said, 'One day you may find out the answers when you meet God face to face, but it can't happen here Judy.' I wrote in my journal a while later: 'So I have to leave that box with God, and in doing so, I'll be more able to identify with others who have their own unanswered questions.'

During this time, my friend Linda also helped me come to terms with laying many things down. We shared a flat in the mid 1980s and had been in very close contact since, although we lived a fair distance apart. When I had first landed on her doorstep in my royal blue cardigan, asking for a room, we had no idea of the life journey we would travel together. Linda is an experienced teacher and a gifted manager, and I often bounced ideas off her. She always made time to listen and suggest ways through my dilemmas. At this time another long-standing friend, Penny, played a crucial role in listening to my thoughts as the knots in my mind gradually became untangled.

Soon after my meeting with the consultant, another friend, Chris, visited for the weekend. She and her husband, Ben, are ordained ministers and have given me tremendous spiritual support. They had been praying for us throughout Russ's illness. Chris encouraged me to take the significant step of moving the mounted photograph of Russ from the lounge to the hall, knowing that I was ready. The next day I rang her to reaffirm my life afresh as a single Christian; I wanted to be open to God's will with all my heart.

Bearing sole responsibility for my children sometimes overwhelmed me. On one occasion, I was driving past a field and noticed a sheep munching away while her two lambs skipped playfully around a tree. I thought about the scene, and sensed God telling me he was the shepherd looking after all three of us. Yes, I had responsibilities as the mother, but he had overall custody as our shepherd. I was also beginning to appreciate that we were complete as a family of three.

I was finding out the vital importance that the girls and I had a balanced routine, especially for our meals and rest. Whenever things went awry at home I could usually trace it back to one of these routines having broken down. Tiredness affected all of us, and even though I'm a fairly patient person and have learnt a lot from life about waiting, when I'm tired I struggle with impatience. Although I didn't have the added pressure of going out to work at this time, there were many other demands on me which left me vulnerable and exhausted. It became clear that as one adult with two children I needed to draw firm boundaries to stay in charge. A neighbour once asked if I was aware that assorted shoes had landed on her side of our back fence the previous day. It didn't take me long to discover that Rachel had told Lucy to join her in getting rid of the shoes, thinking that without shoes they would have to miss school.

On one occasion the girls even packed their bags, but never actually made a run for it! At times like this I really needed God's help and wise counsel. I didn't always succeed in striking the right balance with the children, and sometimes tended to involve them in adult issues. But sharing some responsibilities forged us closely together, and made our relationship even more precious.

The next important step for me in 2003 came at a Care for the Family event, A Different Journey – a project for those widowed at a young age. This event involved a weekend away at a beautiful hotel, attended by twenty or so young men and women also coming to terms with losing a partner. As my mother's health was improving, my parents took care of the children while I went away. It was wonderful to have a break, and I drove there full of hope and anticipation. The couple leading the weekend had been bereaved at a young age, and then married each other. They shared their stories and made themselves totally available to us. I found the whole weekend inspired me with hope for the future.

The lady was a trained Cruse counsellor, and her insights were very helpful. This charity promotes the well-being of the bereaved. I really appreciated being with people who knew what it felt like to be widowed young, and their stories were very humbling. Most of the other delegates were looking for God's help in their grief, and superficiality was quickly swept away as we shared our deepest feelings. I knew deeper healing was coming to me through this process. The evening meal became quite noisy as we all chatted easily together. The next day we enjoyed some lovely walks as a group and I even used the gym!

My next big step was to take the children on a week's summer holiday for single parent families at Lee Abbey, the beautiful conference centre in Devon. We chose a week with a 50 per cent price reduction. As we got nearer to our destination, I realized I was running late and stopped to phone the centre. The countryside seemed desolate, and I needed directions, but my mobile had no signal and I felt totally alone and vulnerable.

Questions raced through my mind: 'Why am I bothering? Why didn't we stay at home? This is all too hard.' I checked the map again and drove on. After a while I sensed my spirit lift, and felt God's reassurance. I tried my phone again and this time got through to the conference centre. They were very kind and helpful; dinner would be saved, and we weren't the only ones who'd been delayed.

We had a wonderful week, during which I became aware that I was moving on from my time of mourning. I heard extremely helpful talks given by Christine Tufnell on Handling Anger in Children and Taking Time for Ourselves, and I very much enjoyed chatting to the team and other single parents.

My other reason for choosing this holiday was to return to the area we'd visited with Russ the year before he died. In some ways I relished the chance to retrace the precious steps we'd taken with Russ, keeping alive the memories for the girls. As I talked about what we'd done there with him – Rachel had climbed the Little Hangman Hill near to Combe Martin, and Lucy had uttered her disgust at the vast array of sheep poo on the ground – it was excruciatingly painful for me, yet also comforting. We revisited a dinosaur park, and it was poignant to explore the same sites and to picture Russ that last summer. I was convinced the holiday was the right thing to do, and that in future these reinforced memories of times spent with their dad would be infinitely precious to them. It certainly felt very natural, and I didn't want these memories to die, to disappear with their father. I wanted to overlay the pain of his loss with a new memory, and to come out stronger. But the return home was more painful than I'd expected. I cried to myself, even though I knew I'd made big strides forward and that I was gently moving on.

That was a glorious autumn, and one Sunday afternoon the three of us went to see the beautiful tree colours at Batsford Arboretum. I missed Russ terribly as we'd all gone together on the previous visit, and the melancholic beauty seemed to mirror the pain in my heart. But once these memories surfaced, they seemed to lose their raw poignancy, and I knew that my next visit would be easier.

As I drove home, the girls were singing in the back of the car. Rachel – who could remember the arboretum and the beautiful photographs Russ had taken with his new camera – was quite peaceful. But in the front, unbeknown to the girls, the tears rolled down my face. It was hard, hard, hard. I had loved Russ so much, and that hadn't changed. But I knew these were healing tears which would help me break through the next barrier. And the next day I did indeed feel much better.

And so 2003 drew to an end. It had brought an increasing sense of closure. Through the events aimed at single parents and the widowed, I'd begun to accept my new status. Prayer had been instrumental in this, as were the kind words of release I'd received from Russ's family. I was pleased that I'd now finished going through the piles of family photographs from before and after Russ's death, producing a chronological history for the girls. My book, too, was progressing, and I was finding release in putting our story down on paper. I looked back with pleasure on the surprise four-day trip the girls had enjoyed to Disneyland with my brother and his family. I carefully recorded all these things so they would be remembered.

Changes were afoot. The following year, 2004, would bring an end to our family business, Huckle's, an old-fashioned tobacconist and hairdressers, which was established by my grandfather in 1921. Built on loyalty and trust, it had run for over eighty years and served the town of Wellingborough faithfully. Another change was the planned retirement of our vicar, who had been with us for eleven years. So the close of 2003 felt like the end of an era, and seemed to coincide with the final steps I needed to tread in my path of grief.

22

THE RAINBOW THROUGH
THE CLOUDS

January 2004 proved to be another tough time. When I returned home after Christmas with my parents, I was shocked to find I was plunged into grief again. I'd really believed that my time at Lee Abbey had brought closure, but once again I experienced the familiar cycle of raw grief, pain and then release. This was another emotionally and physically draining period, but I gave myself occasional treats like a pub lunch or a walk with an old friend, and those helped.

On 22 February I took the girls to the Everyman Theatre to see *Joseph and the Amazing Technicolor Dreamcoat*. The last scene showed Joseph embracing his father after being apart from him for many years. I closed my eyes, longing to be in heaven with Russ, and wishing I were older so that time would come sooner. Then I had one of those special moments when I had a very real sense of talking with God. With eyes wide open, I looked up at the theatre ceiling, and two choices became crystal clear to me.

First: I could coast through the rest of my life, caring for the girls, yet in my heart longing for the time when

Russ and I would be reunited. That choice meant wasting the years ahead. Second: I could wipe any hope of a reunion out of my mind, so I wouldn't have to endure the pain of waiting. And then suddenly I saw a third way, as I sensed God impressing on me that the girls and I were *his* children. I saw that I shouldn't put Russ on a pedestal, and make a kind of god of him, for he also was a child of God. At last I understood that by remaining consumed with this longing, I would miss God's will and purpose for the rest of my life.

When we got home from the theatre, I started searching for Catherine Marshall's book, *To Live Again,* in which she describes a dream where she saw her husband soon after he died. In a dream her husband, Peter, suddenly noticed and approached her. Mixed with the tenderness of his love, she sensed a certain restraint; he was not holding her as a lover. Early on in my grief I could hardly have borne a dream like this, but now I found I could fully embrace it. Peter was holding back and showing Catherine that for her own sake she needed to hold him at a distance, so she could move on with her own life.

Now I understood the futility of waiting for a romantic reunion in heaven, and knew I needed to mourn the end of my marriage. Letting go would release me to enjoy the present fully, and perhaps even consider a future marriage. A whole new way was opening up. My marriage was over. But my loved one lived on, because as a Christian, Russ's death wasn't a hopeless ending–rather, an endless hope.

Over the weeks which followed, I felt as if I was straining to cling to a cloud which was lifting and pulling away from me. In the depth of my grief, my identity had been so caught up with Russ that it hurt brutally to let it go, and in its wake, there was nothing but a growing empty space.

It was then I had a dream in which I clearly detected God's voice. Some friends had asked me to go for a walk with them. When I went to my hotel room to collect my trainers I couldn't get in because there was a crowd of people at my door, all wanting help. Eventually I got in, but then couldn't find the shoes. I began to panic – I'd told my friends I would only take five minutes. All of a sudden, I noticed Russ sitting on the sofa, and Rachel and Lucy were beside me. I gazed at him, gasping, 'You're real. You're really real!' We spent two glorious hours on the sofa as Russ and I embraced, hugged and played with the girls. His countenance was radiant, and I noticed how clean his arms and hands were, particularly his fingernails. When he'd worked on the mushroom farm, his hands were constantly rough and ingrained with soil, so I was particularly struck by these clean hands. I gazed at him as he bent down to pick up a suitcase. As he opened it, several pictures inside the lid caught my eye; they were the kind taken in passport photo booths. They were of Russ, looking very happy, and sitting with other people I didn't know. Puzzled, I asked him, 'Do you realize how painful the last three and a half years have been for us?'

Russ looked straight at me, and replied lovingly, 'I do know, Judy, yes I do.' His empathy showed a real identification with our pain.

Then I noticed, scattered among the pictures, some beautiful snaps of the girls at key stages over the last few years.

When I woke, I felt a glorious sense of peace, and a warm contentment flooded through my body. The timing of this dream – so soon after that theatre trip which had triggered my longing for a reunion with Russ – confirmed in my heart that I was *Judy*, rather than *Mrs Hopkins*.

In spite of these comforting realizations, March blew in another episode of mourning which lasted through to April. Outside the school gates I felt strong, yet back home my legs turned to jelly and tears just streamed. I looked repeatedly for Russ's face at the kitchen window, yearning to see him approach the house on his way back from work. I wanted to be at home, not away, and not at large functions. I needed a gentle touch, peace, healing. It always felt good after I'd cried.

May was tough for Lucy as her little hamster, Chestnut, died. It was very sudden, taking us all by surprise and releasing deep grief in her. I recognized that this flood of emotion was probably her inner pain surfacing – the pain from losing her father as well as the obvious upset of losing her pet. Gazing intently at the lifeless body, she carried Chestnut to show to some of her friends. She wanted to bury him under Russ's tree on Cleeve Hill, and that day coincided with the loss of our cat, Misty, who had been missing for twenty-four hours. The girls were both devastated. I drove us up Cleeve Hill with a heavy heart, wondering if life would ever get easier.

But Misty turned up again, and the year began to improve. I made real progress with paperwork and other urgent affairs that had been pressing on me. My brother visited and helped me sort out the garage, clearing out the old to make room for the new. The girls and I took our stuff to two car boot sales and I even let the baby buggy go. We laughed and said we weren't great entrepreneurs; Lucy made £12 and Rachel spent all she made!

That summer, the three of us spent a week at New Wine in Shepton Mallet, a Christian camp where the last remnants of my grief surfaced, releasing more tears, but bringing with them a new sense of freedom. This time I

was no longer trying to cling to the cloud, and I felt
ready to break out of my chains of grief. In fact, I was so
fed up with the grief that I couldn't take any more of it,
and actively *chose* to leave it behind. Soon after that decision it felt right to move to the larger nearby church,
Trinity, where there were lots of children and I wouldn't
see Russ continually in my mind's eye. God was to
greatly strengthen me there, particularly through the
worship and the inspiring women's ministry, so sensi-
tively led by Karen Bailey.

◆   ◆   ◆

The outline for this book was finished in October 2004,
four years after Russ's death. How wrong I was in my
early assumption that the mourning process would be
over within two years! More than ten years have now
passed since Russ died, and I feel sure God has ordered
the path my grief has taken, and I'm grateful for that.
Since 2004, the time seemed right to leave the grieving
behind, although Russ's memory will remain forever. I
now realize there will always be moments of grief for us;
it will never fully go. I have struggled to accept this, but
in that acceptance I have found peace.

Now, more than ever, I am conscious of a burning
desire to share God's love with others. I can identify
with words from Elisabeth Elliot, whose husband was
one of five men martyred by the Auca Indians in
Ecuador, leaving her to bring up a very young daughter.
In *A Path Through Suffering*,[12] one of her many books
which have helped me, she writes: 'If I concentrated on
my losses and all the very present evidences of his
absence, that permanent, glorious, and solid reward
would be out of focus. I must start concentrating on the
invisible for a change. That was where my treasure was

now, for my heart was there in a way it never had been before.'

Like Elisabeth, I too am deeply aware of a heavenly dimension. Now, as then, I see the rainbow of hope – the symbol of God's promises to his people – eclipsing my cloud of despair. In the first book of the Bible, we see Noah move from despair to hope, as his old life is swept away and he is brought to the place of new beginnings. God sets his rainbow in the clouds, a sign of his binding agreement with Noah, and his people on earth. In the last book of the Bible, John sees a vision of God in heaven on a throne encircled by a rainbow, representing the fulfilment of God's promise through the ages, of his faithfulness to everyone who trusts in Jesus Christ.

Despite all the pain and unanswered questions in our world, there is tremendous hope and a guarantee of everlasting life for everyone who looks to the One who said, 'In this world you will have trouble. But take heart! I have overcome the world' (John 16:33).

Throughout the journey I've travelled with my family, the rainbow has been a symbol of hope to me.

23

THE VIEW FROM THE TOP

Very recently I took a walk alone to the special place on Cleeve Hill where so many of my significant life events have taken place. I don't go up there often any more, unlike the early days after Russ died, when I would walk there repeatedly . . . endlessly. When I began to heal, I deliberately started to avoid the tree, and found a route on the other side of the hill, where a new vista opened up, literally and emotionally.

My recent visit was on a mild February day. Our crocuses were flowering in glorious purple, gold and white under my special tree, and I smiled as I saw the patches of nodding snowdrops that someone else had since planted between our bulbs.

I sat under my tree and looked straight ahead. Close to this very spot, I had stood and looked down on the hospital where I worked as a student midwife, struggling with a painful fear that I would never marry or have children. Near here I had taken communion with a friend after my conversion, and here Russ had cried out to God in desperation after coming off heroin. This was where he had given his life to God.

Below me was the mushroom farm, and I smiled at the memory of Russ's visits to my top floor room, arriving on his mountain bike in our pre-dating days. We would go for pizzas and wonder when our jobs would change, and practise ballroom dancing after work down there in the mushroom sheds. From here I saw the spot where we had watched the Northern Lights together in joy and amazement. And this was where he had finally proposed to me, after all our meanderings as we learned to know and love each other. In this place we both cried – me in grief more times than I can count – both of us on our last night out, a week before his transplant. But even on that visit Russ had let go of my hand and run free. Here his scattered ashes became part of the earth – long ago now.

I thought about how the place was now special to Rachel and Lucy. They had played here after he died, and Lucy had buried her hamster under the tree. Now here I sat, realizing how far I've come. I was wearing my own jacket today. But for two long years whenever I'd come up the hill, I'd insisted on wearing Russ's old green coat, his jumper and shirt. I'd sat in this place wearing his outfit as I planned his story. With a shock I realized I'd been shrouding myself in his clothes just as I was living in the past we'd shared together.

Now I asked myself: 'How am I doing?'

Words which sprang to mind were: peace, settledness, resolution, completion. I can honestly say that I've handled my personal grief now. I still shed a tear sometimes – like when the service sheet for my niece's wedding made a lovely reference to Russ. But my grief is in the past where it belongs. Russ too is in the past – a part of our history which will never change. He is Rachel and Lucy's father, and they're more like him now than they've ever been. He's also very much in the future – alive in heaven – and we will both be in a new heaven one day. But he's not so much in my present, and I don't think of him as he was, breaking into my world of today any more, except to occasionally hurl out the words, 'Look at things now!'

And what of me? I have grown as a woman and I'm not the same person that I was when Russ died. Now I'm free to live my life and walk in my story – and I'm not guilty about that, not in the least. I experience a freedom, and everything is in its rightful place. All is as it should be.

I looked at the nearby path weaving away from the tree, upwards and onwards. That was like my path now. I'm travelling through a different season in life, with new hopes and fresh challenges.

Before I left the tree on the hill, I thought about this book and wondered and prayed about the people who would read it. My story is not unique. Many, many people have travelled similar journeys and have walked through their valley of despair and through a door of hope. I believe this door is open to everyone. Despite all my pain and unanswered questions, I have found new life by allowing Jesus to walk with me along my road through pain.

I was getting cold under the tree. As I walked downhill to the warmth of home, I thought about one grey morning shortly after Russ's death. I was standing in my kitchen, struggling to make sense of a letter from a well-meaning friend, telling me that God was in charge of my life. I was staring blankly at the empty words.

Suddenly Rachel's voice broke through my despair: 'Look, Mummy, Lucy's making her rainbow!' She repeated, this time more brightly and urgently, 'Look again, Lucy's making *another* rainbow!'

To him who sits on the throne and to the Lamb
be praise and honour and glory and power,
for ever and ever!
(Rev. 5:13)

◆   ◆   ◆

Interested in having Judy speak at your meeting?
Please contact her at:
lucysrainbow@hotmail.co.uk

Helen Porter

Helen was born in Warwick and graduated from London University with a degree in English in 1984. As well as providing various other writing services, she has ghost-written the highly acclaimed biography of Fran Burke, *Dying to Live*, and the biography of John Lywood, *Apostle to the Gypsies*. Under the *nom de plume*, Helen Wilkinson, she has also published fiction titles, *The Missing Peace* (2002), *Peter's Daughter* (2003), *Chinks* (2005) and *The Divided Kingdom* (2008). Helen lives near her grown-up daughter in rural Shropshire.

HELPFUL ORGANIZATIONS

Winston's Wish helps children rebuild their lives after the death of a parent or sibling, enabling them to face the future with confidence and hope. It is the largest provider of childhood bereavement services in the UK and offers the widest range of practical support and guidance to children, families, professionals and anyone concerned about a bereaved child. Winston's Wish believes that the right support offered at the right time can have a life-changing impact on bereaved children and young people. The charity provides professional therapeutic help in individual, group and residential settings, and via a national helpline, interactive website and publications.

National Helpline: 08452 03 04 05

Website: www.winstonswish.org.uk

Care for the Family is a national charity which aims to promote strong family life and to help those who face family difficulties. Core activities are in the area of parenting and marriage. Support for single parents includes resources, articles and activity breaks designed exclusively for single parent families. They also provide bereavement support for the young widowed and bereaved parents through events, newsletters, telephone befriending and web resources.

Contact: 029 2081 0800
Website: www.careforthefamily.org.uk

The Harnhill Centre of Christian Healing. Resource for the church and ministry to the individual.
www.harnhillcentre.org.uk

Lee Abbey. Conference, Retreat and Holiday Centre.
www.leeabbey.org.uk

The Alpha Course is a practical introduction to the Christian faith being run by thousands of churches of many denominations throughout the world. They usually serve good food too! For more information about Alpha go to www.alpha.org.

Endnotes

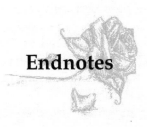

1 Thomas R. Kelly, *A Testament of Devotion* (NY: Harper-Collins, 1996).
2 'Lord, for the years your love,' by Timothy Dudley-Smith (b. 1926). © Timothy Dudley-Smith in Europe and Africa. © Hope Publishing Company in the United States of America and the rest of the world. Reproduced by permission of Oxford University Press. All rights reserved.
3 Steve Biddulph, *The Secret of Happy Children* (London: HarperCollins, new edition 2000).
4 Mary Pytches, quoting from *The Times* in *A Healing Fellowship* (London: Hodder & Stoughton, 1988).
5 'A Fragment of a Prayer' by Peter Marshall, in Catherine Marshall *A Man Called Peter* (Reproduced by arrangment. Grand Rapids, MI: Chosen Books, a Division of Baker Book House, 1951), p. 230.
6 Video produced by International Films, distributed by STL.
7 Corrie Ten Boom lived with her family in Holland in World War Two and offered shelter to persecuted Jews. She and her sister, Betsie, suffered atrocities in Ravensbruck Concentration Camp for offering shelter to persecuted

Jews. Corrie wrote about it in *The Hiding Place*. Corrie Ten Boom with John and Elizabeth Sherrill, *The Hiding Place* (Grand Rapids, MI: Chosen Books, 1971).

[8] Catherine Marshall, *Light in My Darkest Night* (Grand Rapids, MI: Chosen Books, Baker Publishing Group 1989).

[9] Catherine Marshall, *To Live Again* (Grand Rapids, MI: Chosen Books, a Division of Baker Publishing Group, Original 1957).

[10] *Shadowlands* film 1994 produced by Shadowland Productions and Price Entertainment.

[11] Daniel Goleman, *Emotional Intelligence* (London: Bloomsbury Publishing PLC, 1996).

[12] Elisabeth Elliot, *A Path Through Suffering* (Ann Arbor: Vine Books, 1992).